7-2
Bud

I Give You My Life

I Give You My Life

The Autobiography of a Western Buddhist Nun

Ayya Khema

translated by Sherab Chödzin Kohn

Shambhala
Boston & London
1998

Shambhala Publications, Inc.
Horticultural Hall
300 Massachusetts Avenue
Boston, Massachusetts 02115
http://www.shambhala.com

9 8 7 6 5 4 3 2 1

First Edition

Printed in the United States of America

⊗ This edition is printed on acid-free paper that meets
the American National Standards Institute Z39.48 Standard.
Distributed in the United States by Random House, Inc.,
and in Canada by Random House of Canada Ltd

Library of Congress Cataloging-in-Publication Data

Khema, Ayya:
    [Ich schenke euch mein Leben. English]
    I give you my life: the autobiography of a western Buddhist nun/
Ayya Khema; translated by Sherab Chödzin Kohn.—1st ed.
        p. cm.
    ISBN 1-57062-415-1 (cloth: alk. paper)
    1. Khema, Ayya. 2. Buddhist nuns—Germany—Biography. I. Title.
BQ968.H458I2513 1998
294.3'91'092—dc21   98-22143
    [B]   CIP

I dedicate "my life" to Buddha, Dhamma, Sangha, which are my refuge.

Stages

As every flower fades and as all youth
Departs, so life at every stage,
So every virtue, so our grasp of truth,
Blooms in its day and may not last forever.
Since life may summon us at every age
Be ready, heart, for parting, new endeavor,
Be ready bravely and without remorse
To find new light that old ties cannot give.
In all beginnings dwells a magic force
For guarding us and helping us to live.

Serenely let us move to distant places
And let no sentiments of home detain us.
The Cosmic Spirit seeks not to restrain us
But lifts us stage by stage to wider spaces.
If we accept a home of our own making,
Familiar habit makes for indolence.
We must prepare for parting and leave-taking
Or else remain the slaves of permanence.

Even the hour of our death may send
Us speeding on to fresh and newer spaces,
And life may summon us to newer races.
So be it, heart: bid farewell without end.

Hermann Hesse

Contents

I Give You My Life

full Circle

It was a very long way from Berlin, the city of my birth, to here, the Buddha-Haus in the Allgäu where I now live. The two places are actually separated by only nine hundred kilometers, but between them lies my entire life. At the age of fifteen, I had to leave Germany, because the persecution of the Jews going on at the time left me no choice. Today I am seventy-four years old and wear the brown habit of a Buddhist nun.

I have seen and experienced much in those years, and the outer journey that I undertook helped me to find peace and to forgive everything that happened to me and my family. This made it possible for me to complete the circle and to come at the end of my outer and inner journey back to my former homeland.

I have been asked many times by friends, students, and colleagues to write my autobiography. I have always

Childhood years in Berlin.   *In front of Buddha-Haus im Allgäu.*

refused. Nuns and monks are supposed to communicate the Buddha's teaching, not tell stories about themselves.

Now I have finally agreed. I have allowed myself to be convinced that my life story could perhaps serve as an inspiration for some people to enter upon a new way. Leaving external circumstances aside, it is the story of an average woman who for many years moved within a very ordinary mental world, but who was then capable of breaking out of it and emerging onto a new level of consciousness.

My life has been a very adventurous one. But that had nothing to do with me. When I think back now, I realize that I had no influence over most of what happened. The decisions took place without me, and I simply went along.

In this life I have taken on many roles: I have been a very sheltered child, a timid young girl in a foreign land, a girl alone on a freighter to Shanghai; I have been a wife, a mother, a world traveler, a farmer, and now a nun.

For a few years I lived in a very bourgeois style in a suburban house in California with a garden, a garage, and a washing machine in the kitchen.

In the course of a few years, I traveled through half the world: South America, India, Pakistan, Nepal, Kashmir, Hunza. It was a time when I was searching for something that I was at that time unaware of and that I did not then know I would some day find—much, much later.

I worked in a bank in Los Angeles and had a farm in Australia where we raised Shetland ponies. In my opinion, a newborn Shetland pony, which looks like an overgrown poodle, is the most adorable animal in the world.

All that is over now; it is in the past and now lives on only in memory. Probably these many changes and farewells have contributed toward my understanding of the necessity of letting go. For me, a tangible symbol of this letting go was always my hair, which I had to say goodbye to eighteen years ago when I became a nun. It used to be long, thick, and dark; then it was cut off down to the scalp. In the customary fashion, I held a lock of it in my hand for a while in order to contemplate the non-ego quality of corporeality. I put the hair aside without the slightest regret, actually with a feeling of relief. One less attachment.

Now I shall begin with the story of my life, which I have called *I Give You My Life* because I have the feeling of speaking personally to each reader. I hope you will read it with your heart.

Each chapter is introduced by a verse that I believe suits that particular part of my life. The verses are drawn from the *Dhammapada,* a collection of sayings spoken by the Buddha for the welfare of human beings on a variety of occasions. Their wisdom has impressed me many times. I would like to make this story of my life a gift to you from my heart.

March 1997
Ayya Khema
Buddha-Haus im Allgäu

Whatever parents may do for us,
And other relatives too,
A well-directed mind
Helps us still a great deal more.
—Dhammapada, verse 43

Childhood in Berlin

I was born on the twenty-fifth of August 1923. My parents, Theodor Kussel and Lizzi, née Rosenthal, named me Ilse. My zodiac sign is Virgo. Over the years, however, my typical Virgo qualities—diligence, conscientiousness, reasonableness—have transformed more and more into the warriorlike character traits of the zodiac sign Leo. My ascendant is Leo.

The world of the haute bourgeoisie into which I was born no longer exists today. We lived in a twelve-room apartment near the zoo—the best residential neighborhood in western Berlin. We had a cook, a housemaid, a governess, and a chauffeur who sometimes drove me to school. Meals were served by the maid, who wore a black dress with a white apron and a little white bonnet. We had damask wallpaper and velvet-upholstered chairs,

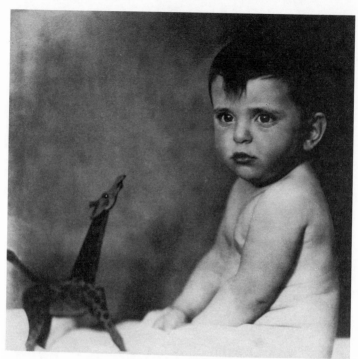

Berlin, 1924.

Persian rugs, and silver tea service. A team of workers came every three months to polish the crystal chandeliers.

I'm telling you this because this atmosphere created in me the feeling that absolutely nothing bad could happen to me: "Everything is splendid; the world is secure and beautiful." I remember this fundamental feeling very clearly. Very soon I was to learn what an illusion it was.

My father was a certified broker on the Berlin Stock Exchange. There were seven brokers there who set the prices of shares based on offers and bids and were thus quite influential. This was a civil service position. Once I asked him, "Daddy, are we rich?" To this he replied, "Well-to-do, almost rich."

One day my father took me on his lap and said something sad: "You know, dolly, we're Jewish." I asked him, "So, is that something bad?" He replied, "Basically, no, but at the moment I'm afraid so." That was the first time the point was ever made to me that we were Jewish, that is, something special. Until that time, nothing at all was said at home about Judaism. My parents were what was called "assimilated." Assimilated Jews no longer concerned themselves with the customs that derived from Orthodox Judaism. They had blended into their environment and behaved, from the point of view of a superficial observer, just like anybody else. Many of them had had themselves baptized and thought of themselves as Catholics or Protestants. In my family we didn't go so far as that, probably because my parents did not consider it important what one's religion was.

They thought of themselves as Germans. My father received the Iron Cross for bravery in the First World War, and he was proud of it. He told me that Frederick the Great of Prussia had let the Jews out of the ghettos. They could live wherever they wanted. In the view of this statesman, everyone should be allowed to pursue happiness in his or her own way. Perhaps this was why the Jews were so eager to blend in with the bourgeoisie. They had a very loyal feeling toward the state, a feeling of gratitude.

I clearly remember my father often saying how wonderful it was to live in peace in a country like Germany. It must have been when I was very little that he said that, for soon it was all going to be very, very different.

My grandfather had a children's clothing store in Berlin, on Rankestrasse at the corner of Taurentzien-

With Grandfather and Grandmother in Marienbad for a cure.

strasse, right across from the Kaiser Wilhelm Memorial Church, which today has become a peace memorial, because the remaining tower of the bombed-out church serves as a reminder of war.

Last year, when after all this time I visited Berlin for the first time again, I looked for this building. It no longer exists. Also I was unable to find the buildings in which I lived with my parents. In a certain way, my childhood has disappeared without a trace. There are no places left that I can go back to. No graves. Maybe this is why the little girl in the few photos I have left seems so remote to me. She is a robust little girl with a round face—I always had red cheeks, I remember that. I still do today.

In front of Jakob Rosenthal's children's clothing store was a droschke stand. A droschke was a kind of horse-drawn taxi. Every Saturday my grandpa drove with me to the zoo in a carriage of this type. At the zoo they used to put on a parade of animals for the children. You could pick out what kind of animal you wanted to ride on. I used to get a ride on an elephant (which I found completely fantastic, because the seat way up high on top of it used to bob around like a ship at sea), or I could ride in a little coach that was drawn by a goat. That was wonderful too. On top of that, they had machines at the zoo that you could put a penny into and get a piece of candy. When we were finished at the zoo, my grandfather also used to take me home in a droschke. Those Saturday afternoons with my grandfather were sheer happiness for me. My mother was his only daughter and I his only grandchild. He was very fond of me and I was very fond of him too.

In his shop he had one of those high desks you have to stand up at, and over it there was a sign that read: "No matter which way you do it, it's wrong." Once I asked him what this was supposed to mean, and he said, "It just means you can't please everybody."

He was a jolly, contented man. When he died, my world got its first jolt. We were at my grandparents' for lunch, as we were every Sunday. After lunch, he lay down for a nap and never got up. I was told that he had gone to sleep. My grandmother simply wasn't able to deal with this. She died two years after him.

"Fortunately," we said later. Fortunately just in time. The year of my grandfather's death was 1933, when I was just ten years old.

For a while I lived on within the bubble of my beautiful illusion of security. If my parents were worried, they

At the State Augusta Lyceum, Berlin 1932 (second row, third from left).

didn't speak about it in my presence. I went to a private school and after that to the state Augusta Lyceum. I had my girlfriends' and my birthday parties as usual, and in our kitchen, as always, reigned our cook, Flora Brambor. I called her Flora Brummbär—Flora Grumblegrunch—because she would never let me enter her realm.

During the Olympics, in 1936, I saw Adolf Hitler for the first time, from very close up. My father had a ticket for all events that took place at the Olympic Stadium. When he didn't have time to go, I could go in his place. It was a very good seat, not far from the Führer's box.

Though I have forgotten a great many other things from my childhood, I still recall every detail of this afternoon. Above all, I still have the noise in my ears of thousands of people shouting "Heil Hitler!" Everybody stood and stuck their hands up in the air. Only I remained seated. As a Jew, I was not allowed to salute him. At the same time I was afraid somebody might drag me out of my seat because I had failed to acknowledge the Führer. But I was still a little girl, so nobody noticed me.

Adolf Hitler saluted the crowd standing up and then said a few words over the loudspeaker. His manner of speaking, his chopped-off way of enunciating his words, and his incredibly powerful and rousing voice magnified my feeling of fear. I felt the menace that emanated from him deep within me.

After the Olympics the government policy toward the Jews became more and more extreme. Jews were no longer allowed to be in the civil service, so my father lost his seat on the stock exchange. At the beginning he was still able to keep working as an independent stockbroker, but his income became very much smaller.

We took a smaller apartment and gave up our car and our chauffeur. On top of this, now Jews were no longer allowed to have non-Jewish employees. That meant that we had to let our cook and maid go. Next it was decreed that Jewish children were no longer permitted to go to the same schools as non-Jewish children. So I was transferred to one of the Jewish schools that came into being in those days as an emergency response to the pressure of the circumstances.

Honestly speaking, the change of schools didn't make that much difference to me. The only thing all our relatives and friends were talking about was emigrating. This was a topic much more interesting than school: were we going to move away, and if so, where would we go? To Czechoslovakia where Uncle Leo lived?

My uncle Leo Kestenberg, who was married to one

of my father's sisters, had been the Czech Minister for Musical Education; thus he was also a government functionary, and had now, for reasons similar to those described above, lost his position. He had been Yehudi Menuhin's piano teacher. He was also supposed to give me lessons. Once we went to his house and he played something on the piano for me. I was supposed to repeat it after him, but I was unable to do so. He declared that I was tone deaf. So I didn't have to take piano lessons.

Czechoslovakia did not turn out to be the right choice—as we know, the Nazis were not long in taking over there. Uncle Leo succeeded in escaping to Israel along with his family. There he founded the Israeli Philharmonic Orchestra. He was one of the few members of my family who survived the persecution of the Jews, he and my aunt Grete and his daughters.

My father took the fatal viewpoint that in the long run, Hitler would not be able to prevail in Germany with his plans to annihilate the Jews. He said that a people that had produced Goethe, Schiller, Kant, and Nietzche, Bach, and Beethoven—such a cultured and intelligent people—would not allow itself to be driven to such inhuman action by any government. He wasn't the only one who was thinking this way. Many people were saying: "Of course, it's all just talk, smoke and mirrors. We'll stay; after all, this is our fatherland; when it comes down to it, we're Germans."

Then came the so-called Jewish poll tax. Officially, this was a kind of tax that Jews had to pay to the state. In actual fact, it was a confiscation of Jewish wealth. I went with my father to the ministry of finance office. As he left the room, he broke into tears. That was the first time I ever saw my father cry. At that moment my sense of security was shattered once and for all. From then on I knew that the world was not safe and sure. I did my best to make him feel better, I remember that vividly. I felt so helpless, and he felt the same way.

We gave up our apartment and moved in with Aunt Wally. She was one of my father's sisters and was married to a Christian. He left her immediately after the "Jewish laws" came into effect. So now we were living there, and one day the janitor shouted up to us from downstairs. Some men with boots were on their way up the stairs, presumably the Gestapo. Since we were the only Jews in the building, we could figure out pretty easily who they were after. My father ran down the back stairs and two buildings over to where my aunt Lieschen lived. She was one of my mother's sisters, and he hid at her place.

On the day after Kristallnacht, when everywhere in the country the synagogues were set on fire and the Jewish businesses were looted, I happened to pass by the burning synagogue in the Fasanenstrasse. I had not been brought up religious, but I knew the square and the building. There was the mob, throwing the scrolls of the Torah into the flames, the Holy Scriptures. A few pious Jews who were compelled to watch this were weeping. It was a shattering experience for me, an unbelievable shock. When I got home, my face was totally white; so much for my red cheeks.

Now it was clear—we had to get away. But it was already almost too late. My father bought a visa for Uruguay that turned out to be counterfeit. When people are in serious trouble, there's a lot of money to be made. That was the same in those days as it is today.

The only country in the world that took in Jews without visas was China. So my father bought two tickets, for himself and my mother, on a ship from Trieste to Shanghai at Lloyd's Triestino. Each ticket cost ten thousand marks. That was an insane price, which took nearly all the money we had left after the Jewish poll tax had been extracted. Arrangements had already been made for me to join a children's transport group going to England, where an uncle of mine lived. England in my parents' opinion was a safer place for a fifteen-year-old girl than the notorious port city of Shanghai.

I accompanied my parents to the railroad station from which the train to Trieste departed. Hardly had my mother reached her compartment when she fainted. I stood outside; my father waved at the window. I would have loved to have fainted myself, I was so afraid being left alone in Berlin.

Aunt Wally was there. She was touchingly concerned about me. There were still a few friends left. But there was also fear—what would happen if the Nazis came to get me? I as yet knew nothing of concentration camps and what went on in them. I was just quite simply scared. Since seeing the burning synagogue I'd had the feeling that the future was something uncertain and horrible. Every day I felt this fear more strongly.

Just to be doing something, I studied Spanish in a language school. I clearly remember my first Spanish sentences: *Nuestra escuela esta en una calle muy hermosa. Tiene tres pisos con muchas salles grandes.*

In April 1939 I finally got a message from the Jewish community organization of Berlin that a place was available for me in a children's transport. I packed a few things—dresses, my favorite children's books. A backpack and a small suitcase were all that was allowed. These could contain no money, no gold or silver—nothing of value at all. In this way nine thousand children were saved; ninety thousand were killed.

Once again a railroad station and a train waiting on the track. We were to be taken first to Hamburg. From there a ship sailed to Dover. I was the oldest of the two hundred children of this transport who climbed aboard with their backpacks and little suitcases. And I was the only one to have to undergo a body search by the police. But there was nothing for them to find.

The children were between two and fifteen years old. Most of them were crying in a heartrending fashion. Their parents were standing behind the barricades; they weren't allowed onto the platform itself. Then it left, this train of tears. The children pressed their faces against the windows and wailed. I didn't cry. I had the separation from my parents already behind me. I had had to leave Aunt Wally behind at the barricades, but by this time that was no longer so horrendous.

I never saw Aunt Wally again, nor a single one of the relatives and friends who remained behind in Berlin. When the war came to an end, I tried to find them through the Red Cross, without success. Not long ago, a memorial book of Jewish victims of National Socialism came out, published by the Institute for Social Science Research of the Free University of Berlin—a mammoth tome of 1,450 pages. There the names are listed, with maiden names for the women, the addresses, birth dates, dates of deportation, the deportation destinations, and, if known, also the dates of death. In most cases, however, the only entry for that is "missing."

I found Aunt Wally in this book. Wally Seidl, née Kussel, born September 27, 1883, in Berlin; address, Stromstrasse 69; transported on March 5, 1943, to Auschwitz; place of death Auschwitz. Missing.

And there too is Aunt Lieschen, at whose house my father went into hiding. Born October 27, 1861, in Gentin, province of Saxony, old people's transport to Theresienstadt. Place of death, Minsk. Missing.

Besides these, I also found the names of many of my relatives and friends. I have no photographs, there are no gravestones. Only this book and my memories.

Every form of existence is transitory.
Whoever recognizes this with insight
is thereby released from suffering.
—Dhammapada, verse 277

Flight into Exile

My whole life long I never felt so lonely as I did on this journey on the train from Berlin to Hamburg. So abandoned by the whole world. At the mercy of a totally uncertain fate. I didn't cry; everything in me was frozen with fear. What a child could lose, I had already lost: my parental home, my family, my homeland. I didn't have an idea in the world of what lay ahead.

Having a homeland is the very essence of a sense of belonging and security. From that moment on, I never again felt really at home anywhere. Familiarity, confidence, warmth—these were all feelings of the past. They had been left behind in Berlin, forever. I have already said that now I am very happy to be living in the Allgäu. That's true, but I'm also ready at any moment to pack my bag and live somewhere else, anywhere in the world.

The idea of "mine" doesn't exist for me anymore—my homeland, my house, my desk. I don't harbor the notion that anything really belongs to me or that I'm entitled to anything. I say that today without regret, because it corresponds to my inmost conviction. The Buddha, to be sure, teaches renunciation of one's possessions, but I was familiar with this feeling much earlier, long before I knew anything about Buddhism.

We sailed to England on a German ship with a German crew. The sailors obviously felt very sorry for all the little children. They were very kind to us and showed us the whole ship, from the theater auditorium down to the engine room, anything to get us to stop crying. They decorated the dining room with paper streamers, and there was even ice cream for dessert. But for the really little ones, this did no good. They wouldn't eat anything and they cried out constantly for mommy and daddy. In our cabin, in which there were six of us, a sailor came every night and told us fairy tales until we finally fell asleep. I will never forget the loving-kindness those sailors showed us. But in the eyes of their government, we were just so much scum.

In Dover, we got on a train for London. There we were met at the train station by a reception committee from the Jewish community. It was composed of about thirty women who were standing at long tables with lemonade, cookies, and sandwiches. Our names were read off from a list along with our destinations: "Kussel, Ilse—Glasgow."

So I was to go to Glasgow. There were two smaller girls who had to go to Glasgow too. We were put on a train by a woman who spoke English. She also gave us a little money to take along, an English pound or two, and a little bag of food.

I couldn't speak a word of English, besides good morning, good evening, please, and thank you. And nobody there spoke a word of German. For a brief moment I found myself thinking that it would have been much better to learn English in the Berlin language school rather than Spanish.

On top of everything else, I hadn't the slightest idea where Glasgow was, even that it was the biggest city in Scotland. At each station I looked out the window to see if this was already Glasgow. Every time I would see a sign that said "Players please." That was the most popular cigarette in England, but of course I didn't know that either. I was amazed that all the towns were called "Players please."

It was cold in the train, and then it got dark, and we rode on and on and on. Then a conductor came. "Glasgow?" I said to him. "Glasgow?" He got through to me that Glasgow was the last stop. My eyes fell shut immediately. It meant that as long as the train kept going, we could remain in our seats.

The next morning we reached the last stop. The family I was assigned to was waiting at the station. The father, the mother, and seven children. They couldn't speak any German; they spoke Yiddish. Since the Yiddish dialect is based on German, they expected that I would be able to speak Yiddish too. Yiddish is spoken in every Orthodox Jewish household, but as already explained, my house was not an Orthodox one.

My host family was of Russian-Jewish derivation. That I was unable to speak with them was a misfortune, but not a big one. The real problem lay elsewhere. They had signed up to take me because they needed somebody who could help the mother in the house with her seven children. But as it happened, they had ended up with the least suitable person for this that could possibly be imagined. Thanks to Flora Grumblegrunch, our cook who would never let me into the kitchen, I didn't even know how to tell whether water was boiling. I was supposed to put pillowcases on, and yet I had never done that in my life. I was supposed to take care of the fire in the open fireplace, but I didn't even know you needed paper to start a fire.

The wife was less and less kind to me; but the husband would say, "Oh, come on, leave her alone; after all she's still a child." They said those things in Yiddish, thinking that because I couldn't speak it, I couldn't understand it either. But I did understand it, because it very closely resembled German.

But in the school I went to every day, I did not understand a word. Where I learned English was at the movies. The least expensive ticket was sixpence, and I was able to afford that out of my meager pocket money. After three months, I spoke perfect English—good enough to be in the movies, you might say.

Being able to understand everything, however, was not purely an advantage. Once when one of my girlfriends from school was inviting me to her birthday party, I understood well enough when her mother said, "This refugee child won't set foot in my house!" These were not the only words of discrimination I had to hear. A boy wanted to take me to a university dance one time. By now I was sixteen years old and had become, I believe, rather on the cute side. His mother said, "Why this foreigner of all people?" He replied, "What makes her different from any other girl?"

What was different about me can be expressed in one single word: I was unhappy. I didn't belong in this place I'd been cast up in. Everything was alien and cold, not only the human side of things but also the weather, which was cold and wet. But I always had a great deal of willpower, and thus had formed an ironclad resolve— you'll hold out for a year, then we'll see; until that time, no whining.

That year went by, and in the middle of it, the war broke out. I wrote to my father in Shanghai, telling him how unhappy I was. "I want to come be with you two," I wrote.

Months went by, and finally in the summer of 1940 the answer came. The first German bombs had already fallen near Edinburgh. My father wrote, "If you're un-happy, then come." By this time, my parents had an apartment in Shanghai. My father had started a ready-made clothing store that was doing well. Readymade clothes were something new in China at the time. Except for the fact that my parents were in such a remote place, everything was okay.

An uncle in London was supposed to get me a ticket on a ship, but it took an eternity. Finally, in November 1940, the ticket came. I told the family I was living with that I wanted to see my parents again. The family took the news that I was planning to leave without wasting a word. Probably they were happy I was going, but they didn't say that either.

My uncle, whom I hardly knew until then, sent me

the ticket for the bus from Glasgow to London. In London, he went about getting me the papers I needed in order to make the journey. After all, I was stateless; the Germans had taken my German passport away.

I still remember clearly: it was evening when I said goodbye to the family in Glasgow. They didn't ask me, "Have you got a little money for the trip?" I walked all by myself in a total blackout to the bus station, carrying the little old backpack and the suitcase I had arrived with. As the front door of the house banged closed behind me, I felt totally lost—an unwanted person without money, without identification papers, alone among strange people in a strange land.

Today I realize that I failed to live up to the expectations of the family. I was unhappy with them and they were also not happy with me. A few years ago I managed to get the address of Mimmie, the daughter of the family, with whom I had gotten along with best. I wrote her a letter and expressed my thanks to her and her family. After all, if they hadn't taken me in, I would have died, like ninety thousand other Berlin children. Since that time, we've corresponded a bit. She finds my life interesting.

The ride of twelve hours it took in those days to get from Glasgow to London was awful for me, because I was terribly hungry. The other passengers were constantly getting out at the various stops along the way to buy themselves something to eat. But I didn't have a penny. In London I had to ask a passer-by for money to make a phone call. That, I realize, is what is called begging. He gave it to me; it wasn't very much.

Thinking about it now, an episode occurs to me

from that other time when I was still a happy, carefree child. I was with my father at the zoo. We were going out through the Elephant Gate and there was a beggar sitting there. I see him clearly in front of me. He had only one leg and held a box on his lap in which he had pencils to sell. My father put a coin in his box, and I thought to myself: That could be me. It could happen to me too—I could be sitting there and begging. I must be a very good girl so that it never gets to that point.

At that time I was about five and knew nothing about religion and of course nothing at all about the Buddha. But what I already grasped intuitively at that time was the teaching of karma, of cause and effect, which I came to know under that name only much, much later. Bad actions cause bad karma. If you do bad things, bad things will happen to you, just like that beggar. It is curious how deep an impression this experience made on me.

My uncle in London was a lawyer. He had emigrated from Germany early on, in 1933; thus he had been more farsighted than my father. He lived not right in London, but fairly far outside it. He explained to me on the telephone how I should get there: he would pay the conductor for my ticket after I arrived. It was a gray morning. I felt immeasurably tired. Everything, every little detail in my life, was beset with difficulties. In point of fact it isn't that easy to convince a railroad employee that your fare will be paid on the other end. Nothing was easy, nothing happened without an effort. I had not yet gotten used to that.

My uncle picked me up at the train station. The conductor got a tip, and for the first time I had the feeling of being expected. It was a wonderful feeling.

I stayed a few days with my uncle and his daughter, my cousin Steffi. At a London office that dealt with foreigners, he got temporary identification papers for me. He gave me a gold cigarette case and a few things of value for my father. And then I was alone in the train again. It was December. The past August I had had my seventeenth birthday.

My ship was in the Liverpool harbor. When I saw it, I got scared. It did not look like the kind of ship one would feel comfortable about taking a long journey in. It looked more like a ship of lost souls out of a pirate movie. It was rusty and dilapidated. It was called *Haruna Maru*. On the deck a Japanese flag flew. After all, Europe was at war. There were no European ships left over for civilian traffic.

The *Haruna Maru* was a ten-thousand-ton freighter, rather a little thing. Japanese sailors were swarming over it. Crates, bags, and barrels were loaded aboard. There were twelve of us passengers—English missionaries, two Pakistani merchants, and an Indian doctor. The doctor was to make me a marriage proposal in the course of our voyage. I was the only young female aboard. It was very hard to get it across to him that at this time in my life marriage was the last thing on my mind.

I remember this voyage as a curious mixture of nightmare and beauty. I had never been at sea before. There was something magnificent about seeing nothing but water and sky, a leaping fish here and there, the rising and falling of the horizon, the changing hues of gray, blue, and green, beneath which you could sense the inky depths. But this was outweighed by the nightmares. Once, in the middle of the ocean, we picked up survivors from a Swedish ship that had been bombed by the Germans. It was a neutral ship, but it had been sunk anyhow. The people were thrashing around in the water and screaming. After that I no longer had any confidence in our big Japanese flag. Who could guarantee that we wouldn't be a target too? At night we sailed completely blacked out. All the portholes were painted black. This slinking through the dark got on the nerves of everybody on board.

It all got to be too much for one sailor, and he ran amok. He dashed around the ship knocking everything to bits. I was in my cabin and opened the door in order to find out what was going on. At that moment he ran at me. He had a broken bottle in each hand and was foaming at the mouth and screaming. Somebody shoved me back in my cabin. The crazed man was overcome and locked up for the rest of the voyage. I cannot forget his face. Since then, I know what running amok means: a sudden derangement of the mind, a bursting forth of inhuman qualities, of horrible animal violence.

Each of the twelve passengers had a little cabin in which there was a bed, a chest, and nothing else. For meals we went to a room where there were little iron tables with little fires burning between them. You sat on the floor on a cushion and roasted fish and raw vegetables for yourself over one of the fires.

I couldn't handle that. I couldn't stand this half-raw food, even when somebody else cooked it for me. I no longer know what I fed myself on during the crossing. Probably crackers and the little fatty cakes that sometimes came out of the kitchen. I was sick the whole time;

I get sick just thinking about it now. That was the worst torture.

And the heat! It was still winter when we sailed from the Mediterranean Sea into the Suez Canal. From then on, it was hot. We stopped in Bombay, in Colombo, one place hotter than the last. I wasn't allowed to leave the ship with the others. My identification papers were not valid as a passport, so I had to stay behind in the small, close ship that lay baking in the sun.

Whoever knows what is genuine as
*   genuine,*
What is not genuine as not genuine,
And is fond of right thinking
Will soon be favored by genuineness.
—Dhammapada, verse 12

The War Years in Shanghai

After Kristallnacht in 1938, a joke made the rounds among the Jews of Berlin: Two Jews were standing in line to apply for passports. One wanted to go to America. "Where do you want to go?" he asked the other one. "To Shanghai," he said. "So far away?" asked the first man. "Far away from where?" said his friend.

It takes a special kind of humor to invent jokes with such bitter punchlines. Jews have a particular talent for it—perhaps because in their history they've had to experience so much misfortune. There are hundreds of emigration jokes that have to do with the horrible misery Jewish people found themselves in. I have already mentioned that Shanghai was at that time the last refuge for the European Jews. Most countries had shut their borders.

In a rickshaw in front of our house in the French Sector, 1942. My father is in the background.

Uruguay sent a big ship full of emigrants—or immigrants, depending on what side you look at it from—back to Germany. America and Australia were taking in only selected individuals.

Because of a British-Chinese accord dating back a hundred years, Shanghai was an open city, which required no entrance visa. Between 1938 and 1941, twenty thousand Jews took refuge there. It was far from home, but not far enough, as we were soon to learn.

My parents were waiting below on the quay when the *Haruna Maru* pulled alongside. A stone—no, ten giant boulders—fell from my heart when I saw them. My father had on a black coat, the same one he used to wear in Berlin. With my baggage, in which the anxiously guarded gold cigarette case from my uncle in London was secreted, we climbed into two rickshaws. It was very cold; through the streets of Shanghai blew the icy wind off the

Mongolian steppes. In spite of this, the two rickshaw coolies pulling us were sweating so profusely that steam was rising off their bodies. I could never get used to being in a conveyance drawn by people. I learned that the coolies did not live a long time; they literally worked themselves to death. But that's the way it was in Shanghai. No one could change it—at least not me. I was glad when the first bicycle rickshaws came in.

We rode to the French part of the city. Shanghai at the time was an international free port with a French, a British, an American, and a Chinese quarter. I found it a terribly ugly city on this winter day, with the exception of the broad avenue along the shore where the English had built their banks and commercial buildings.

Our rickshaws stopped in front of a handsome apartment house. I climbed up the stairs with my parents, my father opened the door, and I walked into an apartment with furniture from Berlin. Somehow my parents had managed to have a few chairs, paintings, and Persian carpets sent to them by ship after they left. It was quite an unreal sight, these familiar things here in a foreign place.

Together with three other Jewish emigrants from Berlin my father had opened a ready-to-wear store for ladies' fashions. It was an elegant store next to the Palace Hotel, and it was doing very well. The ladies of Shanghai were completely wild for off-the-rack European clothes; there had never been anything of the sort here before. Moreover, I got to be outfitted in Daddy's store. The little skirts and blouses that I had taken with me from Berlin to Scotland and Scotland to China had gotten too short and too tight.

I had no school degree, no diploma, nothing. My

With my parents in front of our house in the French Sector, 1942 (before the Japanese Occupation).

father sent me to a Shanghai business school. "You'll profit from it your whole life long if you learn how to type," he said. That was very farsighted. Even these days, I sit every day working at the typewriter. And because I also learned bookkeeping and shorthand, I was later able, for years, to earn my family's living.

In the afternoons after school I went to play tennis. For a short time in Shanghai I was able to be young and carefree once again.

In December of 1941 the war in the Pacific began. The Japanese conquered Shanghai, among other places. In February of 1943, they put out a proclamation: The European refugees—that meant the Jews—were to be confined to the part of town known as Hongkew: a ghetto without walls but with barbed wire, under the control of the Japanese military authorities. This was the result of German pressure. The Japanese were Germany's allies, and for the Nazis, Shanghai was not too far away to keep the Jews there from being persecuted along with those elsewhere.

For us it meant giving up our apartment and our business. My father now lost his livelihood for the second time. I believe this had a very profound effect on him. After all, he was no longer a young man.

We rented two rooms in Hongkew and took our furniture and carpets with us. We still had a bit of crystal too. It was from the sale of these things for the most part that we were able to feed ourselves.

During this time I learned that even in the most adverse circumstances, life goes on. In our ghetto, with approximately eighteen thousand inhabitants from Germany, Czechoslovakia, Poland, Austria, and all the other countries in which Hitler ruled, there arose a little community with a hospital, a school, a theater, Viennese cafés in which you could get Sacher torte and apple strudel. We had a newspaper and a kind of social welfare service for children and old people. The child mortality rate in Hongkew, on account of the inadequate hygiene and because hardly any milk was available, was very high.

I left the ghetto every morning and came home every night. I had a job with an export company. All my earnings I gave to my father. We lived very frugally. There was a soup kitchen that we could go to. What was cooked there was tasty, but it was always the same: kasha soup with a few vegetables swimming around in it, and with it we got bread that old people were unable to eat because it was hard as a stone. On holidays we would buy twenty grams of liverwurst or an ounce of coffee. We had to pay insane prices for those things.

My father had a map on the wall on which he marked the progress of the Allied troops with little pins. We were forbidden to have a radio. But young boys had built their own radios and hidden them under their mattresses. In that way we could still get news about the course of the war. We were able to get an idea of where the Americans were and when this nightmare might come to an end for us.

One day bombs fell on our ghetto. There was a loud boom and I went out a few steps in front of our building. Next to me was somebody I knew, and all at once it was as though he was swallowed by the earth. An explosion, a gigantic crater, and the man had disappeared. At that point I became hysterical, the one time in my life. I was screaming and couldn't stop until my father gave me a slap. "There is nothing more we can do; now be quiet!" he cried.

And I was quiet. Never again did I fly off the handle like that—it's not my style. But this experience was too much for me. I was standing next to someone, and before my eyes he was reduced to microscopically small pieces. He had been a musician in one of the Jewish cafés. I used to enjoy listening to him play.

A lot of bombs fell that day; a lot of people were killed. In the street in front of our house, blood flowed like rainwater. The American pilots were trying to hit a Japanese radio station and had missed their target.

Perhaps it was in connection with this experience that I completely lost my fear of death. Since then, I have never worried about whether I was going to live or die. One moment a person is there, the next moment gone. I learned that very early.

In August of 1945, before the atom bombs fell on Hiroshima and Nagasaki and the war came to an end because of the terrible consequences, my father began having pains. The doctor who examined him diagnosed kidney stones and said the stones had to come out. My father went into the hospital. Naturally, conditions were not optimal, but we all felt that he would make it through. On the day he was to be operated on, he got a mild fever. The operation was postponed. The next day I visited him. A doctor took me aside and said, "Your father is not going to be able to get through this alive." In the hospital he had caught encephalitis, an inflammation of the brain tissue, from a Japanese soldier who had been brought there in a mortally ill condition. There was no remedy for this. There was as yet no such thing as penicillin.

I went into my father's room. He was lying in bed and he was very weak. He knew he was going to die. Every dying person knows this. He was fully conscious. I said to him, "Daddy, I'll be right back, I'm just going to go get Mommy." Then I ran like a mad person all the way home, with tears streaming down my cheeks.

Back in the hospital, I tried to give him a few spoonfuls of soup. He couldn't swallow anymore. He was completely calm. He said that I certainly knew already how much he loved me and that he wished me all the best for my life. Then he also said he would continue to watch over me.

I was completely unable to deal with this. I simply could not believe that he was dying—just a few days before, he had still been in good health. His was the first real death for me. That other death during the air raid had also been a shock, but after it my father was still there standing next to me telling me to stop screaming.

For me my father was the mainstay of my life. I stood outside in the corridor while my mother said good-bye to him. A few friends also came. Then he was dead. I couldn't cry. It took me a long time before I was able to cry.

Five days after that, the war was over, which particularly upset me, because my father had longed so passionately for the end of the war, and now he hadn't lived to experience it.

My mother was as though paralyzed, capable of nothing. I had to take care of everything, the funeral and the continuation of our lives. The Americans occupied Shanghai. GIs distributed candy bars. But even they couldn't provide us with an apartment. We had to stay on in our miserable two rooms.

Two years earlier, because of the Japanese, we had lost our business and the greater part of our possessions. I made an attempt to get compensation for our losses, but it turned out to be hopeless. Everything was simply gone.

A few months later, my mother married again, a friend from her youth in Berlin who also lived in the ghetto. From that point on, I was completely alone, without a father and without a mother—for of course she gave all her attention to her new marriage. I was unable to understand this. I thought she should have given herself more time to get over my father. Today I see it from another angle. My mother was a dear woman, but very unstable and fearful. She couldn't stand on her own feet in life, like many women in those days. She needed someone to protect her.

I was twenty-two and quite pretty, if I may allow myself to conclude this from a photograph of myself that I have from those days. It is a considerably retouched photo; I have unnaturally long eyelashes in it. But you can see anyway, that I was a good-looking young woman. One day I met a man who was seventeen years my senior. He was also a Jew from Germany; his first name was Johannes.

It's possible that he represented a father substitute for me. Friends and acquaintances were of the opinion that he didn't suit me. I didn't have that impression—I married him. We moved into a tiny apartment in Hongkew. There was electric light, but the only water was down in the rear courtyard. For heat we had a little charcoal stove. I never succeeded in lighting it; as a result it was always cold at our place in the wintertime.

My husband ran a shirt factory with a cousin of his, and it did very well. I found a position as a secretary with the American army of occupation and was making two hundred dollars a month. That was quite a lot of money in China, enough to feed a family of twenty. So things were going better for us. I was allowed to shop at the PX, the store for the American military personnel. There were wonderful things there, like toothpaste, for example, and white soap that had a wonderful odor, and ice-cream powder. I was able to afford an *amma*, a Chinese servant.

*At the age of
nineteen.*

From her I learned a little Chinese, the Shanghai dialect
that no one outside that city understands a word of.
When my daughter Irene was born in 1947, the *amma*
was a big help. One of the main things she did was wash
the diapers in the rear court, which was very difficult and
labor-intensive work.

Nearly all the Jews who lived in the camp wanted to
go to America. The Americans were willing to take us in,
but the bureaucracy took its own time. The voyage to
America took place on troop transport ships, and for
what seemed like forever our turn didn't come. My
mother and her husband were able to make the journey
before we were.

Finally Mao's soldiers were on the edge of Shanghai, just about to take the city. Then at last our turn came. We left Shanghai on the last transport ship in 1949. Those who were unable to take that ship were arrested by the Communists. So I was lucky. I had been lucky before too: in 1939 I had been on one of the last ships that took children out of Germany.

Troop transport ships of that type held roughly fifteen hundred to eighteen hundred people, men and women separated. We were six mothers and six babies in one cabin. It seemed as though the children had come to an agreement to cry by turns, never all at once. So it was utterly impossible to sleep.

But we were on our way across the Pacific! We were on our way to San Francisco! I remember the first time I saw the Golden Gate Bridge and how very beautiful it looked appearing out of the fog in the morning sun. On the dock a band was playing the well-known song "San Francisco, Open Your Golden Gate."

Once again a new life was beginning. How many times had it been already? I had gradually learned, like one of those round-bottomed punching dummies, to keep coming back to my feet. I was now twenty-six, a woman with a husband and child, still without a passport but with a little bit of money saved up. Sometimes I had the feeling that this situation would never come to an end: keep your head above water, grit your teeth. For what?

"These children, this money is mine."
The fool torments himself with such
thoughts.
One does not possess even a self of
one's own,
How then children or money?
—Dhammapada, verse 62

New Ways, New Worlds

June 1949. It was ice-cold when our ship pulled alongside the dock in San Francisco. That was normal, because it is nearly always cold and windy in San Francisco. We eighteen hundred Jews from Shanghai stood at the railing crying for joy, but with our teeth knocking together. Below on the dock—just as it was ten years ago in London—women of the Jewish community organization were waiting for us, about four hundred of them. They had put up tables among the warehouses and freight hangars and were handing out hot coffee, sandwiches, and cookies. And again there were the lists with the addresses of the places where we were to be put up.

They were touchingly concerned about us. This was connected with the fact that Jews in America had been unwilling to accept the truth of the reports from Germany. They had simply been unable to believe that in that country people were being killed en masse. Now they knew it was true, because their own soldiers had opened up the camps and had seen the inconceivable things that had been going on there.

We received a slip of paper with the name of the hotel where a room had been reserved for us. In addition, we received seventy dollars a month for food. In those days, you could do quite well with that. They had also thought of clothing, for in fact we had little else besides what we were wearing. The community had gathered clothes for us, both secondhand and new. We could pick out whatever we liked.

The garments were heaped up in a huge hangar. Never again have I seen so much clothing in a single pile. We particularly picked out warm things: sweaters and coats. I also took a handbag. When I opened it up, I found a ten-dollar bill inside. I went to the woman who was supervising the distribution and tried to give the money back. No, she said, it was intentional. Whoever ended up with the handbag also got the money. That made me feel rich and especially well cared for. I still remember that with a feeling of gratitude. It was almost like a little miracle.

I began to look into the whereabouts of my relatives in Berlin. I went to the Red Cross. But there was no indication that any of them had survived. They were all dead. Already back in Shanghai I had seen how many Jews, especially those of the older generation, were consumed with hatred for the Germans. I could understand this; the Germans had taken away everything they had. But I was unable to share their feelings of hatred. I still recall thinking at that time that they were ruining their lives with their hatred, the vestige of their lives that remained to them.

There is a verse of the Buddha: "No fire burns like greed; no grip grips tighter than hatred; no net entangles as much as delusion; no current compares to the current of craving." And the Buddha also said that hatred can never be eliminated through hatred, only through love. At this time, I still knew nothing of the Buddha. Nevertheless I experienced things that way. It was clear to me that it was essential to be reconciled and to forgive. After a while, I actually succeeded in achieving this, even though I continued to hear many more things about the atrocities the Germans had committed.

I thought to myself: It's over. Only the loss of my father was a pain that would not go away. In Shanghai I had taken a picture of his gravestone, but to this day I have still never been able to find this picture. In the course of my many journeys and changes of residence, most of my pictures and papers were lost.

So now we were in America, the land of freedom. There was just one person in the United States I knew, a girlfriend of mine from school who lived in Los Angeles. Our host from the Jewish community organization advised us to go to the East Coast where employment conditions were better, but I wanted to go to Los Angeles. We were given tickets on the Greyhound bus to Los Angeles, already paid for, and I quickly found an apartment in the immense city. It was a very tiny one, one room only, much too small for a married couple with a child. But it was not expensive and it was furnished. After all, we had no possessions beyond the little bit of money we had saved in Shanghai. But with that we had enough to pay the rent for the time being.

My husband found a job as a cutter in a shirt factory. It was badly paid, but it was regular income for all that. I roused myself and went out looking for a house for us that we could buy with a small amount of money down and monthly payments. The house we finally bought was not large, but it had a garden in which Irene, our little daughter, could play. I was happy. For the first time, we had four walls around us that nobody could force us out of. We had a real living room and a kitchen with electric appliances, and the water, unlike in Shanghai, was not in the courtyard. Once, many years later, I drove by that house. When I saw it, I thought, "Goodness me, how little it is!" But in those days, it was a wondrous thing to me.

I got myself a job. It wasn't that hard; after all, I was a trained secretary. The Bank of America in Los Angeles hired me immediately. Then I got my driver's license and bought myself a car, an old jalopy that wasn't destined to keep running much longer. In it I drove all the way across Los Angeles to my job. I still remember with horror the first time I drove to work. In Los Angeles, even then, the traffic was hellish. The driver's seat was soaking wet when I arrived at work; I had perspired that much from sheer excitement and fear. But for all that, I came through in one piece.

The atmosphere in the bank was actually discriminatory toward women, as it would be expressed today. The upper floors were all occupied by men. I took Irene to kindergarten every morning. She wasn't very fond of it, but there was really no choice. My husband got seventy cents an hour for his work in the shirt factory. Of course that was nowhere near a sufficient wage. There-fore there was no alternative but for me to work as well. When my child was sick, I had to be at my desk on time regardless. In cases like that, my mother came to our aid. By this time she was living in San Diego with her second husband. It took her about an hour and a half by car to get to Los Angeles.

When my husband's company moved to San Diego, we all moved there. Then in San Diego, my boy Jeffrey was born. At this time Irene was already almost ten years old. I had always wanted to have a second child, but the doctors said that I couldn't have any more children be-cause I had a tumor. When I became pregnant, my doctor was quite irritated. It was completely impossible, he said. As it turned out, Jeffrey was born within a half hour, without any complications whatsoever.

After that I stopped working. Now my husband was making more money, and I had two children to care for. Irene was going to high school; I was on the parents' council. I took care of all my responsibilities, keeping ev-erything in proper order in the house and the garden. I was busy from morning till night, which is quite normal in those circumstances. I got a great deal of pleasure out of the work in the garden, but of course I derived the most satisfaction from the normal and healthy develop-ment of my children.

Nonetheless, quite gradually, something was stirring in me, which in the beginning I experienced as a very slight pain—something that showed me in a scarcely per-ceptible fashion that something was not right. I had ev-erything I could wish for. All the same, something was missing. What it was, I myself did not know. What I had

In America, 1960.

was a vague feeling of incompleteness, an inner malaise, a longing that kept getting stronger.

I was thirty-four years old. So much had happened, and now, all of a sudden, everything that fills the life of most people seemed to have been achieved. I couldn't form an idea of how things ought to go on. Should they just go on in the same way? Was that all there was? Or was there something that lay beyond meeting the needs of everyday life?

There must be something! I began to read a lot—philosophical and spiritual books, whatever I could find. Much I didn't understand, but that did not intimidate me. I thought to myself, "Eventually, I'll get to the bottom of what they're saying." The nonmaterial side of life is what I was occupied with; that is what I wanted to get a meaningful understanding of, to make a connection with.

With these ideas and feelings, I was entirely alone. I knew no one who thought the same way I did. Every time I brought up this type of subject at home, my husband would lose his temper. "What is it you want?" he would ask, upset. What did I want? A new kind of human life, a way of living that related to my innermost heart. But I had no idea how to approach this idea of mine.

One afternoon during this period I visited my mother. In her living room lay two bicycles, entirely taken apart. "Are you planning to open a repair shop?" I asked her. "No," she said, "the bikes belong to the boys out in the backyard." "What boys?" I wanted to know. "You know them," she said. "In Berlin, they always went to the same children's birthday parties you used to go to. Hänschen and Gerd. Hänschen is the son of my best girl-friend, and Gerd is his cousin."

I could only remember Hänschen, and him only vaguely. He was a few years younger than I, and, as we know, among children that is quite important. He had emigrated from Berlin to England, where an uncle of his had taken him in. He had then been a soldier in the British army and had found his parents again in Theresienstadt, where, as a German-speaking officer, he had been posted. Then he emigrated with them to Canada.

Gerd had gone via the children's transport to Glasgow, just like me. Both his parents were killed in Auschwitz. In Glasgow, just as in Berlin, we had both gone to the same school, but we had never knowingly met each other. Later in Glasgow, he had studied electrical engineering, after I had already gone to Shanghai. Now, having completed his studies, he was cycling through America with his cousin Hänschen from Canada.

Life takes its own strange paths. In Buddhism, we speak in cases like these of karmic links, but I knew nothing of such things yet. Now, in my mother's house, I met Gerd. And though we didn't have an inkling of it yet, a new life was beginning for both of us. At our first meeting, we already saw that we were both on a similar quest for meaning in life. We understood each other amazingly well, because we shared this deep longing.

This encounter gave me courage, because now I knew someone who thought the same way I did. I tried to make suggestions to my husband about what I could do to pursue my search. But every idea I came up with fell on deaf ears. He didn't want me to change and he didn't want our life or anything else at all to change. Because of this attitude of his, our relationship got into such a rut that I decided to risk the big step of facing things on my own, that is, of separating from him. Things could not continue the way they were. That was not going to make either one of us happy.

When I told my husband I wanted a divorce, he was outraged, furious. He has never forgiven me for leaving him. He also could never understand how distant we were from each other in our innermost needs.

It was a terribly difficult decision for me. Irene was thirteen, Jeffrey was three years old, and our house was the first real home I'd had since my childhood.

I left everything just as it was—the house, the furniture, the books, the car, the clothes. Irene stayed with her father in San Diego, partly also because this was where my mother lived. She had to finish school. I took Jeffrey with me and moved to Rancho La Puerta in Tecate, Mexico. This was a farm being run as a health spa one-and-a-half hours from San Diego, right on the United States border. The director was Professor Edmund Szekely, who had written more than seventy books on physical and mental health. At the farm he taught the philosophy of the Essenes and gave courses on natural nutrition and life style. The Essenes were a Jewish sect that flourished at the time of Jesus Christ. They had rules for their order which, among other things, prohibited private property and marriages. They were vegetarians and extremely pacifistic, in contrast to other Jewish sects.

It was an utterly fascinating place. Many interesting guests gave talks at the ranch, for example, Aldous Huxley. The guests on this health farm were people who were looking for more than just saunas, solariums, and vegetarian cuisine, although all those things were offered there too. They were looking for spiritual nourishment.

There I began my first focused study of a spiritual teaching. I subscribed to the periodical of the Self-Realization Fellowship (founded by Swami Yogananda), which was sent monthly and included talks and question-and-answer sections. I was happy to have found people with an outlook similar to my own, even if only on paper. Despite the distance, it conveyed to me a sense that someday the thirst I was feeling could be satisfied.

The most profound truth I learned only much later. Nevertheless, I learned a great deal at the Rancho La Puerta—from Professor Szekely, from others who gave talks there, from the Self-Realization Fellowship, and from guests and fellow workers. It was a new world that

With Gerd at Rancho La Puerta.

opened up to me there, one that was stimulating and inspiring to my mind.

I worked half days as secretary to Edmund Szekely's wife. In exchange for that, we received room and board, a woman to take care of Jeffrey (from whom we learned Spanish), and pocket money. Irene visited us on weekends. To Gerd, I wrote enthusiastic letters.

A year later he came to the ranch too. He worked half days at the reception desk, which he enjoyed and which occasionally even brought in tips. Then we decided to get married. The wedding took place on a mountain behind our little house, with lots of Mexican workers as guests, with a rabbi, with Jeffrey and his little dog. The dog got at the wedding cake, I remember that. And I also remember that I found everything very romantic. Our life was carefree and beautiful.

For my divorced husband, there was a happy ending too. He went to Germany (I was able to help him with the arrangements) and undertook a search for a girlfriend of his youth whom he had lost track of during the Nazi period. He actually found her. She moved back to America with him, and he has been happily married to her for almost forty years. He is eighty-nine now.

I don't find these private things so much worth the telling, but they belong to my development and show that for a long time I lived the same life as many other women, with the same problems and entanglements, and with the same risks that are always involved in separations and changes. It takes courage to face those things, but they can lead to total freedom.

At Rancho la Puerta, all three of us became vegetarians and have remained so to this day. I became very interested in health and nutrition, and I read and learned a great deal there. The ranch was gloriously beautiful, surrounded by vineyards and vegetable gardens. It had a swimming pool, arbors under large trees, and an immense fireplace around which we often used to gather in the winter. Here I heard a great deal about the relationship between body and mind, between life style and spirituality.

I still knew nothing of Buddha. I only knew that there was something within me—a vibration, a resonance, a higher ideal. I couldn't even put a name to it yet. But the feeling was there, and it was wonderful for me that Gerd felt the same thing. However, at that time we still thought the most important thing was a healthier and simpler life style and believed that this would lead us to inner happiness.

Jeffrey at Rancho La Puerta. Everyone in the family became a vegetarian.

We lived at Rancho La Puerta for two years. Then Gerd came to the conclusion that the time had come for us to have a look around Central and South America. He is an adventurer and very fond of new things; even today he often takes trips. I also was no stranger to this inner unrest. Sometimes I thought it was connected with the fact that we had lost the security of our parental homes at an early age. We were incapable of relating to any place as reliable home ground where we could sink roots. We were at home nowhere and everywhere.

So we bought ourselves a Willys Jeep with four-wheel drive. We had received some compensation money from Germany. What's more, by then I also had an American passport. It was a very special feeling to be an American citizen, a person with normal rights, after all those years of being stateless.

We refitted the Jeep in such a way that we could sleep in it. And then we embarked on our journey—first to Mexico. But it was to take us much further than that. Jeffrey came with us. Irene stayed in San Diego. She was now sixteen, with the university a year away.

Soon after, she began her studies, but she didn't finish them, because she got married when she was eighteen. She married a friend from school who was also eighteen years old. Neither one of them had a job, and of course everybody was against the marriage, including me. There is no way this can work out well, we all said.

However, it turned into a very successful marriage, one of the few marriages I know of that really work. From that it can be learned that we have to let our children go their own way. We have to let go. That is a lesson that I came truly to understand later, in connection with another situation.

We are guests on this earth and cannot possess anything—even what is dearest to us.

Those who are mindful set forth,
They take no delight in any abode.
Just like a swan leaving a marsh,
They leave one home after another.
—Dhammapada, verse 91

Departure: Central America by Jeep

While we were still living in Rancho La Puerta, we were once visited there by a group of scientists who had observed an almost extinct tribe in the jungles of Mexico, trying to understanding how these people lived, what they ate, what drugs they took, how they treated their illnesses, what rituals they performed. Now we wanted to undertake a voyage of discovery of this very nature.

Our Jeep had four-wheel drive. Gerd had built a big box on the roof to hold our luggage. On the inside, in addition to our bed, we also had a camp stove.

We were an unlikely set of traveling companions—a man, a woman, and a little boy. In those days, the backpacker kind of tourist you run into everywhere today didn't exist yet. In 1961, when we started our journey,

The Jeep is our home.

foreigners were still a complete novelty for many natives. People gaped at us, but everywhere we were treated with kindness. Jeffrey probably had a lot to do with this. People who have a child with them can be depended on not to have anything nasty up their sleeve. From the very beginning, he was far more of a help than a hindrance.

I should state in advance that our trip lasted far longer than we anticipated. Our original plan was to settle down somewhere in the country. This is something we did do much, much later, but not in South America—in faraway Australia.

Jeffrey was always there with us. Now and again he attended kindergarten, depending on when we happened to stay somewhere for a longer period of time. Most of the time I worked on his lessons with him myself. Today he is a computer specialist at the University of Brisbane.

Only once during the whole time did he become seriously ill. That happened as a result of his drinking bad water. Apart from that, he was always just fine. He was a real little warrior, very independent and full of confidence. There was no need to keep a constant watch on him. He participated in everything without complaint, and he ate everything that was put in front of him.

There were no hotels during this part of our journey. Once or twice we stayed overnight in an inn. We always bought our food in the marketplace and prepared it ourselves. Jeffrey was an enthusiastic partner in the shopping. His Spanish was impeccable, and he bargained with the market women like a professional. Because he was so little, they gave everything cheaper to him than they did to us. To this day, he loves to go shopping, but he can no longer speak Spanish. He has completely forgotten it. He has completely forgotten that the people called him Jeffrito, "little Jeffrey." No matter, we forget our previous lives too.

To begin with we drove down through Mexico to the Yucatán Peninsula, where the Mayas and Aztecs had their temples. We took quite an interest in the everyday life of the people of their bygone age. For example, we studied the excavated sites with a view to learning what we could about how people used to get by without machines and electricity; or how people were able to make pottery and other utensils at home.

Then we got to San Miguel de Allende, a city founded by the Spanish conquerors because there were silver mines nearby. Today it is a national monument, a very beautiful city with a university where the teaching is done in English.

In San Miguel de Allende for fifty dollars we rented a five-hundred-year-old house that belonged to an American. It was completely equipped, up to and including two servants and two dogs. One of the dogs was an immense Great Dane, the other a little white Pomeranian. The Great Dane was extremely timid; at night, at the slightest noise, she jumped in bed with me. Every time she did this she almost crushed the life out of me—she was not only big, she was also fat.

The house had a wall along the street with a gate in it and an inner courtyard containing a well and a multitude of tropical plants. It was typically Mexican and quite beautiful. So we stayed there and began attending the university.

For the first time in my life, I was at a university. My husband had completed a degree, but I had always had to deal with the practical side of life. It gave me great joy to study and to learn. I took courses in creative writing, photojournalism, history, and of course Spanish. This is a beautiful language in which I am still somewhat fluent to this day. Back in Shanghai my father had told me that typing would always be a needed skill, and he was right. What I learned at the University of San Miguel de Allende also turned out to be highly practical. In many places along our way, I wrote articles for American magazines, and I not only took the photos that went with them myself but also developed them.

Jeff went to a kind of kindergarten run by Catholic nuns. He didn't take to this at all—he was used to his freedom. One day he came home beaming with happiness. I asked him what had happened that was so wonderful. "Oh," he said, "the head nun died and we got the afternoon off. Isn't that great?"

But by that time our stay in San Miguel de Allende, the city that silver built, was just about over. After two years of being in one place, my husband felt that it was time to move on and have a closer look at the rest of Central and South America. As always, I went along like a good wife. I was having fun too, and everything was very interesting. But I was never the driving force.

Just about this time the Pan American highway was being built. It was not yet finished; in particular, there were still no bridges. We drove the Jeep on this highway from Mexico to Panama. Every few kilometers we would come to a river. It was always the same story. A few yards before the river, there would be a piece of wood lying in the road with the word *desvio* painted on it. *Desvio* means "detour." This was a joke, because there was no detour. There was the river in front of us and we had no choice but to drive across it in our four-wheel drive car.

Some of the rivers were shallow, but others were pretty darn deep, with swift currents. Of course, I was mortally afraid. Jeff was completely without fear; he thought the whole thing was great fun. But one time, we really got ourselves into a dangerous situation. We got stuck in the middle of one of the rivers. Gerd walked back the way we had come and got hold a couple of road workers. He gave them some money and they hauled us out of the river with a winch. That was the only time we needed help. Except for that one time, we always managed on our own.

In Costa Rica we went through an earthquake. We were spending the night in a little inn when suddenly the room began to wobble and shake. I grabbed Jeffrey out of bed and raced outside with him. Nothing more happened, but that was my first experience of an earthquake.

It is extraordinarily unpleasant. But Jeff slept peacefully through the whole thing.

I have particularly pleasant memories of El Salvador. There were many waterfalls with ponds at the bottom of them in which we could swim. Everywhere there the people we met were very kind to us. We got to know Catholic missionaries and farmers of Indian descent. In every village we would go into the marketplace so we could talk with the inhabitants—that is, if they could speak Spanish and not only their own dialect. We were curious how they lived, because we still were planning to live our lives far away from the world of technology and the civilization we were used to.

After four weeks of strenuous traveling, we reached Panama. There at the post office dozens of letters were awaiting us—messages from another world. Panama is separated from South America by the jungles of Darién, which were impassable to a car. There were expeditions that were able to make their way through this obstruction, but for us getting through it was impossible. I don't know if even today the road goes through there. So we left our car behind and took a plane to Bogotá, Colombia. Bogotá is the capital with the highest elevation in the world, 2,645 meters above sea level. I was walking down the street there, and suddenly I was no longer able to breathe. Yet I was in the best of health! It was reassuring that Gerd, who always made a point of his robust health, was also out of breath. One had to get used to the altitude. Only Jeff was unaffected by the extra couple of thousand meters of altitude. He was hopping about as usual.

From Bogotá we went by bus to Quito, Ecuador. The bus was full of chickens and people. Officially, there were seats for forty people on the bus, but there were at least eighty people on board. People were sitting and eating and chatting, the chickens were cackling, gobs of hot sauce were falling from pieces of bread, and through it all, the bus driver drove like a madman. All South American bus drivers do this. They drive at insane speeds but not at all well. They take their attention from the road to give every young woman they pass the once-over. At such moments, they express their manhood by pressing down extra hard on the gas, causing the goats and geese by the side of the road to scatter in panic-stricken flight.

I have to admit that I did not find this bus trip particularly pleasant. However, I didn't have the confidence to say so, because Gerd was totally thrilled. He loves challenges. When he sees a high mountain, he has to climb it. I myself prefer to stay at the bottom. Today he is sixty-nine years old and hasn't changed. He's still taking bus trips of the same sort.

We arrived in Quito intact, which to my mind bordered on a miracle. I was completely done in, covered with dust, chicken droppings, and hot-sauce stains. We took a room and had a wash, and then we decided for once to spend the money to have dinner at a good hotel. But they refused to let us in, because Gerd didn't have a tie on. That's the first thing that always comes to my mind when I think of Quito.

From what is dear, care comes,
From what is dear, fear arises:
For those free from what is dear,
There is no care, how then fear?
—Dhammapada, verse 212

The South American Adventure

The words of Buddha quoted above moved me particularly deeply. At the time I am writing about, I was still a young woman and was not acquainted with them; even if I had been, I would not have understood them. What does that mean: "those free from what is dear"? Today I know that that does not mean that one shouldn't love. It only means one shouldn't be too attached to dear things, especially dear people, in such a way that one worries incessantly about them. I was far from free from this kind of attachment in those days. I was in a continual state of worry. The journey we were on was not one of those taken under the protection of baggage insurance, health insurance, and the kind of insurance that covers your trip home in case you get in trouble—we weren't traveling the way people like to travel these days.

We were risking a lot. But it was precisely on account of this, in situations that were right on the edge, that I began to understand what letting go means. Being free from what is dear means not clinging, not trying to direct and determine everything that occurs. It means acknowledging that dear things and dear people also exist without me—and that I also exist without them. It was still going to be a good while before I began work in earnest on this insight, but it was during this time that it began to emerge.

But now back to Quito, our first stop in South America. In Quito we heard of a tribe of people that were called Los Colorados, "the Colorful Ones." This was a small tribe in Ecuador that was well known for its herbal medicine. Come what may, we wanted to get to know the Colorados. Therefore, in spite of my fears, once more we got on a bus and rode into the mountains, where, according to what we had been told, we would meet members of the tribe in the marketplace of a small town.

This trip was even worse than the last. It was a narrow road, just wide enough for one vehicle, very curvy, with a vertical rock wall on one side and a sheer vertical drop on the other. The driver drove recklessly, frequently turning around when a child would scream inside the bus or a bird would fly by outside. That lasted three and a half hours. I kept asking myself what would happen if another bus came in the other direction. Thank heavens, none came.

The little town that we finally arrived at was called Ciudad de Colorados, City of the Colorados. And indeed we immediately saw a few "colorful ones" in the marketplace. From the waist up they wore no clothes, the women included, but only had blue stripes painted on their bodies. Around their hips they wore skirts, the men short ones and the women long ones, also with blue stripes. On the heads of the men were little hats of brilliant red.

We engaged two of them in conversation. I asked the older of the two what his hat was made of. It was so bright I couldn't identify the material. "What hat?" he asked. The fact of the matter was, it was his hair. And this turned out to be the special identifying mark of the Colorados. They rub the red juice of a certain berry into their hair until it becomes quite gummy and can be shaped so that it looks like a helmet. Married men leave it at that. Unmarried men fasten an additional tassel made from cotton wadding onto the top of this coiffure, so that everyone—mainly every woman—can see that they are still available.

I wanted to know how often they had to renew this hairdo. They turned out to have a very practical approach—they were expected to produce a fresh coiffure only every half year. We took photos of them together with Jeff, and at that point they offered to take us back home with them. We rode in a little cart that had a small horse hitched up to it. It was a somewhat bumpy ride but it was significantly more pleasant than the bus.

The Colorados were an Indian tribe that was close to extinction. At that time, there were only five hundred of them, all living in this village and the surrounding area. They gathered the herbs that they had been familiar with from time immemorial and used them as medicines. Their young people were moving into the city. They didn't want to be herbal healers like their ancestors, but modern urban doctors. They wanted to make money and also no longer wanted to walk around with red hair caps with tassels hanging off of them.

We were received very kindly by the families of our hosts. They lived in very beautiful houses that were built on stilts. The airy spaces under the houses were filled with hanging bundles of herbs. The people had names for them, but only in their own language, which unfortunately we could not understand. Thus we were unable to take back with us any of their mysterious knowledge about the workings of plants. We have to figure that in the years that have passed since our encounter with them a great deal of that knowledge has simply been forgotten. The younger members of the tribe, the elders told us, wanted to live differently. They wore jeans, not the blue-striped skirts of the Colorados. That was the rage in those days. For a pair of jeans, one could buy nearly half a village.

They invited us to eat. They set before us the most magnificent of fruits. These were papayas that were blood-red inside, the likes of which I had never seen before. There were also red bananas and steamed rice with vegetables. They kept chickens and ate their eggs. When the chickens got old, it was their turn in the pot. The Colorados were not hunters. They were a totally peaceful, unassuming little nation.

Our visit with them made a deep impression on me. I can see before me the grandmother roasting bananas for us over the fire. What has happened to them all? It is profoundly disturbing to take in such a clear impression of completely inevitable changes like those these people were about to undergo. Perhaps the little village with the houses on stilts simply no longer exists. Perhaps the herbs have long been growing wild with no one to pick them.

From Quito we took a plane to our next destination, Lima. Everything in me rebelled against the idea of taking another bus trip so soon. True, we had to be frugal, to save our money, but all the same, just to recuperate, I wanted to sit in a plane again.

In Lima we rented an inexpensive hotel room, as our accommodation on four wheels, our beloved Jeep, had been left behind in Panama. In the weeks that followed, I often found myself thinking about the Jeep, how well we'd slept in it and how valiantly it had transported us, even through rivers. That had been challenging enough, but a mere trifle compared with what awaited us now.

From Lima we wanted to get to the Amazon. For that we had to take a bus over the Andes. As we climbed into the rattletrap vehicle—it seemed as though it might be held together with thongs—we were struck by the fact that all the natives traveling with us had brought a piece of lemon with them, which they were constantly sniffing and licking. By the time we learned what the lemon was good, it was too late.

The bus chugged uphill to an altitude of 4,700 meters. At that level you get altitude sickness: that is, you begin to feel ill and you get bad headaches. For that, as the natives knew, lemon is a good remedy. We were able to buy a few of them, but by that time we were already so sick they weren't of much use anymore.

We reached peak altitude in bad condition. The bus driver called for a short rest stop. Our fellow travelers ate chicken and corn cakes. Then we went down the mountain to Pucallpa. Pucallpa is depicted on the map as a city,

In the paddle-wheel steamer in the Amazon region.

but it is only a busy, large, somewhat hapless village on the Ucayali River. Further along, the Ucayali comes together with the Marañon River to form the Amazon.

We wanted to travel down this river and then further on, down the Amazon. And in fact we found a steamer that was to sail downstream in a week. It was a paddle-wheel steamer, the last that still plied the Ucayali. It was fueled by charcoal and had a huge wooden wheel that turned slowly. We booked a cabin on this ancient ship.

The trip on this ship could not be described as comfortable. The steamer had to pull ashore every day to have fresh charcoal shoveled aboard. There was a shower for the passengers, but it could not be used, since that's where the turtles were kept, which one after the other were boiled for our meals. The turtles needed water; that's why they had been quartered in the shower. Quite apart from the turtles, the food that was put before us each day was more or less the most frightful I have ever consumed. Thank heavens, we had a few provisions with us, and in addition, there were bananas that were quite delicious.

But the worst thing was the water. The ship's cook simply took it out of the Ucayali, which of course was used by all the people on the banks and in boats as a toilet. That's what our tea was brewed with. From this water Jeffrey became mortally ill. Fortunately, I had prudently brought some antibiotics along. Without these, he surely would have died. From that point on, we didn't drink another swallow of that tea without tossing some of the disinfectant tablets, which I had also brought along in my travel pharmacy, into the pot.

Once Gerd was about to take a bath in the river. Everybody began to shout, "Piranhas, piranhas!" These are small fish with razor-sharp teeth, which make their appearance in the hundreds. They can reduce a swimmer to bones in the shortest possible time. They didn't catch Gerd—he climbed the rope ladder back up into the ship as fast as he could.

Whenever charcoal was loaded aboard, we went on shore and had a look around in the pitiful villages that were there. A truly indescribably misery prevailed in these places. This had nothing to do whatsoever with picturesque nearness to nature. All you saw was filth, disease, and malnutrition.

And then one morning, our paddle-wheel steamer ran aground on a sand bank. We had just passed the point where a second river, the Marañon, flows into the Uyacali to form the Amazon. Our captain was drunk, as he al-

With visitors in our barn in Orellana in the Amazon region.

most always was, and so it was no wonder we had run aground.

Piranhas or no piranhas, everyone on board jumped into the water and tried to push the steamer off the sand bank. But it wouldn't budge. Obviously the news of the event had spread in the settlements along the bank like wildfire. Little boats began descending on us from all sides. The passengers, who gradually were reaching the conclusion that no further progress down the river was going to be possible with our steamer, climbed one after the other into the little boats. It didn't matter where the boat was going, just as long as it was going somewhere.

We hesitated for a long time. Then we too climbed into a tiny boat and were paddled to a village called Orellana that cannot be found on any map. In this Orellana, in the Amazon basin, we spent four weeks. I wrote an article about it for an American magazine with photos in which I always appear in a Mexican skirt and a white blouse. Apart from a pair of black corduroy pants, those were the only clothes I had. I had to keep washing them constantly, because obviously there was no possible way of carrying further wardrobe in our backpacks. By the way, the article bore the title "Full Moon over the Ucayali."

Orellana could not really be called a town. It consisted of twenty houses and a church. There were only two men in the town with any authority: a Spanish missionary and the owner of a sawmill. The sawmill owner was rich; he even had a car. He told us that he was a Jew and his son was studying in Glasgow. He could speak English. It was a totally unreal encounter in this remote corner of the world.

In Orellana there was no inn where one could pass the night, so the sawmill owner put an empty barn at our disposal. He was also willing to let us have as much wood as we wanted. Gerd was able to build beds out of planks. We had sleeping bags, which we laid on the plank beds, and those were our sleeping arrangements. Since the barn had no windows, we had to leave the door open all the time. The word had gone out that some foreigners had arrived. The total child population of the locale—I think there were about forty of them—showed up and stood all day long in our doorway so they could watch what we were doing. This was not particularly pleasant; we had no private life at all.

We found out that there was a kind of restaurant in Orellana where it was possible to get a meal. We went there every day and ate mostly fish—we had to fill our bellies one way or another. The fish was fresh-caught and had a wonderful taste. In addition we made friends with the missionary. He took us with him into the jungle and showed us butterflies of a size that you cannot see anywhere else. They had a wing span of half a meter and were truly gorgeous colors. We also saw snakes that were quite beautiful—long, thick, and multicolored. We didn't get too close to those.

The missionary told us that deep in the forest were head hunters who went out on war parties every few years and cut off the heads of their defeated enemies and dried them. When he saw how horrified I was, he let me know that it had not been a long time since they had completed such a campaign and that they were not likely to be out and about on such business again any time soon. That was his idea of how to calm my fears.

Later we saw dried shrunken heads in the tourist shops in the cities of the Amazon. They were about the size of an apple and had really tiny faces with eyes and hair. You could buy them for exorbitant prices. We passed on that one.

Every day word came that our paddle-wheel steamer was going to start again on its trip downriver. But this actually never happened. Then we heard that another large ship was going to come and pick us up. That ship actually did come, but it sailed on by without stopping. Finally we reached the conclusion that we were never going to get anywhere just by waiting. We had to take matters into our own hands.

We rented a boat, which was a hollowed-out tree trunk with a small outboard motor and a little tin roof. You could sit under the roof to avoid being burned by the

*Hair washing in
the Amazon.*

murderous heat of the sun. This boat was to take us to
Iquitos, which was the next large town along the banks
of the river.

The Amazon is not a calm and gentle river. Traveling
over high waves in a hollowed-out tree trunk was quite
frightening for me. I was especially worried on Jeff's account. But the boy played with his little cars or searched
in the water for fish. He was having a great time, quite in
contrast to me.

Every evening we had to go ashore to sleep, because
there wasn't enough space in the tree trunk. Every evening it was the same: drag the boat up on the shore so
that it wouldn't float away; go inland to get away from
the mud of the bank; and build a fire to protect ourselves

from the mosquitoes, which reach the size of horseflies there and are a terrible plague.

For firewood there was always driftwood lying around. Our boat owner was very efficient—he was capable of making even damp material burn. As long as the fire kept smoldering, the mosquitoes stayed away. When we fell asleep and the fire went out, they went on the attack. Thus our nights were not exactly disturbance-free.

During the day we often had to stop somewhere to get hold of something to eat. That was very difficult, because the people themselves had nothing. They would have been happy to take our money, but for the most part they had nothing they could sell us. Sometimes there were a few bananas or papayas. Only once did we come upon a bakery that produced real rolls. Somehow or other, we succeeded in feeding ourselves.

After a week, we reached Iquitos. The first thing we saw when we climbed out of our tree trunk was a man who was leading an animal on a leash. It was an animal for which we had no name, an animal with a shaggy coat and a very long nose. It was in fact a coati, a small variety of bear with a snout used for burrowing, whose habitat, as I later read in an encyclopedia, is in the warmer parts of South America.

"Warmer" was not exactly the appropriate word for the insane heat of Iquitos. We paid off our boatman and dragged ourselves and our baggage to a small, inexpensive hotel called the Hotel Peru. "Notice, now," I said to Jeff as we set ourselves up in somewhat civilized conditions for the first time in weeks, "that the hotel has the same name as the country we're in."

Before looking for a restaurant, we marched off to the post office to send my mother and Irene a telegram. It had been forever since they'd heard anything from us, and they certainly must have been worried. It was an old-fashioned post office with high wooden service counters, which I (being by no means tall) could barely see over the top of.

When I turned around, Jeff was gone. He was not with Gerd either, who was in the room next door, mailing some letters we had written along the way. He was also not in the plaza in front of the post office. He had disappeared as though swallowed up by the earth.

The next hours were one long nightmare. We ran through the city in the murderous heat, asking every person we met if they hadn't seen a small European boy. Nobody had seen him. All the streets in Iquitos end in the jungle as though at a wall, and in the jungle there are snakes and other wild animals.

I was almost faint with fear. Gerd went to the police and told them we'd lost a little boy. The policeman asked, "How old?" "Five years old," Gerd answered. "No," said the policeman and continued cleaning his fingernails. "And you," he asked, "how old are you?" In that instant we gave up all hope. We left the policeman sitting there and went back to our hotel. And there was Jeffrey sitting on the couch in the lobby. He greeted me reproachfully: "Mommy, where have you two been this whole time?" He had been sitting there for four hours and had explained to the owner of the hotel that his parents were lost. After he had been unable to find us in the post office, he had asked a passer-by to take him to the hotel that had the same name as the country we were in.

Today he can't remember this incident either. I, on the other hand, remember every minute of it. "From what is dear care comes, from what is dear fear arises." I think that it was on this day that I began to come close to the teaching of the Buddha within myself—in ignorance of it, it's true, but with growing readiness.

We remained for a little while longer in Iquitos. Gerd had his hair cut there by a barber who had the second profession of taxidermist, somebody who stuffs animals. In his "studio" there was a live anaconda, which he proudly showed Gerd. As soon as he had time, he said, he was going to kill it and stuff it.

The anaconda is the biggest snake in South America. It reaches about six meters in length and has a girth of about sixty centimeters. It is very beautifully colored. The back is olive green and black, and the sides are speckled pale and dark yellow. Gerd looked at the snake with mixed feelings. Supposedly an anaconda eats not only capybaras but also humans. But for the barber, there was nothing all that special about the anaconda.

From Iquitos we flew back to Lima. We could have taken another steamer—the trip was supposed to last two weeks—but after our experiences on the Amazon, we no longer had the level of confidence suitable for this. Who knew where the steamer would get stuck this time?

From Lima we flew to La Paz in Bolivia and from there to Brazil. We skipped Argentina. In Brazil I had relatives, to whom we paid a visit. They were stunned and totally speechless—they thought that I had died in Germany.

In Brazil, Portuguese is spoken. Up to that point, I had been of the opinion that the difference between Portuguese and Spanish would not be great enough to pose an obstacle. But I could not understand a word of Portuguese, and nobody there spoke a word of English either. Thus the situation was quite difficult. All the same, we were in Rio and so we went to see and admire Sugarloaf. On the beach at Copacabana we bought Jeff a big kite, which he happily ran back and forth with. We then traveled on to São Paulo, intending from there to go on to Brasilia. This was the new capital of Brazil, freshly hacked out of the primeval forest; it was supposed to be very much worth seeing.

But before leaving for there, we made a quick trip to the American consulate to pick up our mail. There we were advised to leave the country as quickly as possible, because a revolution had just broken out in Brazil. Owing to our difficulties with the language, we hadn't taken in this information at all. So as soon as we could, we flew to Panama, where our car was waiting for us.

Our next destination was Australia. Already some time ago, we had bought tickets for the voyage on a passenger ship of the Pacific & Orient Line. At this time, the Australian government was highly accommodating. It wanted to attract immigrants to the country and had paid our passage there, including our car. We had only to add ten pounds sterling of our own. That's the way things were in those days, owing to the tremendous loss of human life during World War II. Nowadays, Australia is just as hard for immigrants to get into as Europe or the United States.

Did I really want to go to Australia? At that time I thought, why not? After all, I did not feel truly at home anywhere. So what reason was there for not going to Australia? Indeed, for a long time we had harbored the idea of buying a farm somewhere and living a self-sufficient life in the country.

The crossing was a dream. Because of the food, I quickly put on five kilos. The ship was fantastic: there was a swimming pool, there were board games, sitting rooms, theater presentations—every comfort was available. Naturally we had booked tourist-class accommodations, but nevertheless we had the feeling of living amid the highest level of luxury, especially after the difficult weeks we'd just been through. At one point there was a two-day layover in Tahiti. A more magical spot on earth I had never seen. There were beautiful people, flower garlands, guitar music on every corner, and the air everywhere was incomparably sweet and fragrant. This is the way I imagined paradise. I thought of the painter Gauguin, who had indeed sought and found paradise here. But in spite of that, he had not been happy.

I would gladly have stayed in Tahiti, but that would not have worked. The island was a French territory, and the French were not as receptive to guests as the Australians were.

The next port of call was Auckland in New Zealand. Since we were told that our ship would put in again at Wellington a few days later, we decided to rent a car and cover the distance on land. In this way we saw something of New Zealand. What we found was a wonderful green South Sea island, inhabited for the most part by white people who were especially friendly and forthcoming and who clearly felt a sense of well-being in this place. We were told that here three million inhabitants were nourished by the wool of thirty million sheep.

We visited a settlement of Maoris, the original inhabitants of New Zealand, who enjoyed the same status as the white settlers and had never suffered persecution. Knowing this also contributed to the peaceful feeling that we had in New Zealand. We saw beautifully carved ornamentation on the houses, and loud and joyous native dances.

The greatest attraction of New Zealand is its magnificent lakes. These are turquoise blue or green and black in color, depending on the characteristics of the local soil. There are also hot springs everywhere that send steam up out of the ground. The most famous are in Roturua, where the healing springs are open to the public. There is hardly a place in New Zealand that is without steam. Almost every hotel has its own spring. The water that comes out of the ground is so hot that the springs have to be fenced in so that people don't come too near and burn themselves. In many places steam and water rise up out of the earth like a volcano. In the old days, the Maoris used this water for cooking.

In Wellington, we met our ship again. Upon our arrival in Sydney, we did not land alone. The crates containing all our possessions, and naturally also our Jeep, landed with us. We immediately had a good feeling on the new continent—and we were totally equipped. Now I no longer had to keep washing my second blouse and Gerd's second shirt for the following day.

Initially we were able to live and eat free in a collective camp, which was quite generous. However, we did not want to stay in Sydney but wanted to get out into the country. So we climbed into our Jeep, which was after all also our apartment, and drove hither and yon all through

Australia. We drove along the beautiful east coast with its miles of snow-white beach, empty of human beings. Then we drove west into the interior. This is an area of desert. There are no people around, and animals are seen only seldom. Once we encountered a herd of wild horses. Aside from that, there were occasionally kangaroos and huge flocks of galahs, pink-gray parrots that made an incredible racket.

This was November, and November in Australia is boiling hot. After three weeks of the heat, I'd had it. We recuperated for a few days near Alice Springs in a motel with air conditioning. Anyone familiar with Australia knows that such a trip is an extremely strenuous undertaking. It has to be well planned, because water and gas are only available in places that are quite far apart.

We took a look at "homesteads" on the immense land holdings. The biggest property was supposed to be the size of the state of Texas. We saw children receiving their schooling over the radio. We drove into a reservation where the aborigines live, the original inhabitants of Australia. They live a double life, half according to their own customs, half according to those of the white settlers. Many of them earn a little money by selling souvenirs to tourists: small hand-carvings, imitations of their totems and boomerangs, which we bought from them. Each article cost "two bob," two shillings, even though this unit of currency had long since ceased to exist.

We drove our Jeep via the great Stuart Highway from Darwin, the northernmost city down to Adelaide. When we got back to Sydney, we had a definite idea of where we wanted to settle down. The region we had liked the most was in the southern part of Queensland, an hour

north of Brisbane, the capital, in the vicinity of Nambour.
At that time this was quite a small town; today it is a big
place. This is the area where we wanted to look for a
farm.

But things turned out quite differently, as so often
happened in my life.

If you meet someone who points
out your faults
As though revealing hidden treasures,
Who is wise and reprovingly sets you
straight,
You should stay in the company
of such a wise one;
For whoever keeps the company
of such people
Will be better off, not worse.
—Dhammapada, verse 76

On an Island in the Indus

I n Sydney there was a telegram waiting for us. The
telegram came from a company that Gerd had once
worked for as an electrical engineer. In the telegram
he was offered a two-year contract in Pakistan. As far as
the money was concerned, it was a very good contract.
As for the job itself, it was a killer. A power plant had to
be built at a point on the Indus River where there was
already a dam.

We quickly decided to accept this contract. The project fell within the framework of the Colombo Plan, a
development plan that had been signed by the major

industrialized countries in Colombo, the capital of Sri Lanka. It committed these countries to carry out major industrialization projects in the not-yet-developed countries, and to furnish everything needed, including personnel and materials. The power plant on the Indus was a project of this nature being financed by Canada.

Before we could leave, we had to present our situation to the Australian authorities and explain to them that although they had paid for our passage to Australia, we now wanted to go to Pakistan for two years. The authorities were cooperative. We had to deposit the sum they had laid out for us at a bank. In two years, upon our return, the sum would be paid out to us again.

This is exactly what took place. Although it took us five years to come back, we did get our money back. The Australian government was tremendously generous in those days, and we were exactly the kind of people they wanted: an electrical engineer with a wife and a small boy who could be trusted not to shrink from whatever difficulties might arise.

We were not travelers in the real sense of the word. Travelers leave home and at some point return home again. As for us, we were globe trotters, nomads.

We booked our flights from Australia to Pakistan (which were paid for by Gerd's firm) in such a way that we could make a little detour to Israel. Gerd had once lived for a period of time in Israel, spoke perfect Hebrew, had been an officer in the Israeli army, and had many relatives there. What could be more obvious than that we should spend a few weeks seeing Israel?

All the biblical sites came to life for me. I felt a new sense of connection with my Jewish heritage. Archaeologically, Israel is a true treasure trove. Everything recalls to the onlooker the country's adventurous past.

After that, we flew to Karachi. Pakistan greeted us with nearly inconceivable heat. The city of Sukkur, in Sindh, to which we first drove when we left Karachi, lay in the middle of the Sindhi desert. At that time Sukkur had about a hundred thousand inhabitants, but it was not a city in the sense that we were familiar with; it was just a collection of houses built in a sea of dust. The second hottest place in the world is just thirty miles from there. The hottest is in the Sahara.

From Sukkur we drove to the site of Gerd's job, on the Indus River. There we learned that there was no place for us to live; we didn't have a roof over our heads. All the same, the company was very happy that they had found someone in Gerd who was prepared to work in this remote place. There were not many engineers who were willing to accept such conditions. After all, most of them had wives and children who wanted to remain in their houses and schools and with their friends and relatives. As happy as the company was about our coming, they had made no preparations for us whatsoever.

A future colleague of Gerd's had already arrived before us, without his family. He had rented himself a room. What we should do, he too had no idea. As he saw it, we just had to look around.

We looked around and met some English engineers who had just repaired a bridge over the Indus and were now packing up to leave. On an island in the river, they had had two elongated buildings built, composed entirely of single rooms. This looked like a primitive motel layout. They were willing to let us take over the two buildings from them. So we went ahead and set up household in the various rooms, with quite satisfactory results. There was a bed and a set of shelves in each room. Whatever else we needed had to be bought in Sukkur.

And then the staff that had been planned for us arrived. The company had made an agreement according to which the Pakistani government had to pay our servants. Nobody asked us anything—they simply all moved in with us: a cook, a bearer, a sweeper, a dhobi (laundry-man), machinists for the generators that were there, and three watchmen, who were supposed to watch over us in eight-hour shifts. All of them were paid by the government. We had to take them whether we wanted to or not.

Our cook was a jewel. He had worked in an English household, called me "Memsahib," and cooked marvelously. A "bearer" is a houseboy. He serves the food, washes the dishes, and when he's working, wears a gold-colored turban on his head. The sweeper's job was to keep the place clean—that is to say, relatively clean if you didn't look too closely.

Our dhobi, who was supposed to do the laundry, was a catastrophe. He ruined all the clothes. The laundry is done there in a very unique fashion: the article to be washed is made wet and then beaten against a stone until it is "clean." Nothing ever got really clean, especially since, in addition, there was no such thing as a clothesline. Clothes were dried by laying them out on the ground. One piece of laundry or another was always being ruined. On several occasions I wanted to let the dhobi go, but then he threw himself on his knees and pleaded with me to keep him on, since he had "seven smalls." That meant seven children. Of course I didn't fire him.

Our watchmen were also nothing to brag about. One night we were awakened by a pitiful cry of "Sahib! Sahib!" and a pounding on our bedroom door. There stood our night watchman with his knees knocking, asking Gerd to come with him right away. We were able to infer from his blubbering that there was a gigantic cobra outside the kitchen door. Gerd told him that in point of fact it was the watchman who was supposed to deal with things of this nature. But he only cried out "Master!" over and over again. So Gerd went to the kitchen door, where in truth there was a cobra raised up on its coils. He chased it away with a couple of well-aimed stones. We never saw the cobra again. During the action, which lasted a good half hour, the watchman hid in the kitchen.

In addition, we had a chauffeur. It's true he was unable to drive the little open army Jeep that we had been given in Pakistan (our own having remained behind in Australia), but he could speak Urdu, the language of the country, and Pushdu, which is more common in northern Pakistan. Thus he became our interpreter and also felt himself to be our protector.

Thus we set up our domestic situation. I had school material for Jeff sent from Australia. There they not only have a radio school for children in remote settlements, but also a school that operates through the mail. I was properly and regularly served by that school in Pakistan. Every morning I did schoolwork with Jeff. That was not an entirely simple business, since he was not happy about sitting still with me to do his lessons. But then he finally did go along with it, primarily because he enjoyed reading and writing.

After we'd been living there for some time, we sent

him to a Pakistani school so that he would have contact with other children. He learned Urdu there, but as the only foreigner among seven hundred children, he was dreadfully unhappy. So we soon took him out of school again.

Gerd had been assigned an office—and a secretary who had no idea how to do her job. The upshot was that I took her job and thus also became an employee of the company. This was not a bad solution, because it raised our family income, and Gerd got the professional help that he urgently needed. Besides, other than that, I didn't have very much to do.

So I trained myself in the specialized field of overland electricity conduction. Gerd's work was to design the power line network, do the necessary surveying for it on the ground, and then draw up the plans that would be followed in putting it in place. Also, the power plant to be connected to this network had to be designed by Gerd in every detail. Then he had to figure the costs and requisition the material. The plant was to be driven by the water of the Indus, which had already been dammed. Building materials worth many millions of dollars were delivered on the backs of camels. This was quite a comical sight. We took pictures of those camel caravans, because it is not very often that you get to see modern technology transported on camel humps.

Our island was connected by bridges to both banks of the river. One bridge spanned the water separating us from Sukkur and the other continued on to Rohri, the next neighboring town.

Every morning the sounds of the muezzin's cry reached us in our house. Muezzins are mosque functionaries who intone the call to prayer to the believers from the top of the mosque's minaret five times a day. Nowadays in Muslim cities, this is usually done by playing a tape recording through loud speakers. But in those days you still got to hear real voices, and they sounded marvelously beautiful. I listened to them as I looked out my window with wonder at the camels and donkeys plodding over the bridges, who with their bells sounding, contributed further to the Oriental atmosphere.

In addition to their significance for traffic, the bridges also had another function. Since they formed the connection between two cities—Sukkur and Rohri—they were a preferred spot for beggars. Dozens of them lay and sat along them in a long row, stretching out their mutilated arms or legs at passers-by and asking for alms. I often saw local people giving a coin to every single beggar.

I was completely at a loss how I ought to behave in this situation. Since Gerd and I crossed one of the bridges every day more than once, and since the beggars looked horribly pitiful, miserable, and desperate, I had the urgent desire to do something for them. On the other hand, it was hardly possible to distribute dozens of coins several times a day. I took my problem to our cook and asked him what he thought the best solution was.

He made a clever suggestion, which we followed during the entire period of our stay. He told us it was the custom for well-to-do people to invite the members of the beggars' guild of their city to a festive meal once a month. He told us he would look after procuring the food and cooking the meal. When I asked him about the beggars' guild, he explained that this was a kind of union with a president and other officers, and that every beggar was assigned his precise begging station by this guild. Then he pointed out a particularly pitiful-looking beggar and told us this was the president of the guild and a comfortably well-off man with several houses in Sukkur.

How would the beggars find out that we wanted to prepare them this meal on a particular day? He assured me that it would be fully adequate for him to announce this in the bazaar. And that's precisely the way things happened. On the designated day, about five hundred beggars appeared, chattering gaily, and dug into the repast our cook served up for all of them. He had worked on it the entire previous day, and there was not a single crumb left over. This seemed truly to be the right solution, for whenever we crossed the bridge, the beggars waved at us in a friendly way and in my heart I was relieved.

In everyday life, my experience with household staff as a child in Berlin now came to my aid. It was not so alien for me as for the wives of other foreign engineers to give instructions to staff. The other wives often became desperate over the problems of having to organize their many servants. This was actually not easy. You had to look after everything. Our chauffeur's daughter was supposed to get married, and I had to give him advice about the dowry. If one of my "team" was sick, it was up to me to get a doctor. When the servants had a dispute among themselves, it was my job to settle it.

I often thought back to the difficult times at the camp in Shanghai, where I had been so poor. Now we suddenly had enough money; I was practically affluent again. I had a flock of servants and could really buy myself whatever I wanted. But I had no idea what I should buy. Once again the feeling arose in me that there must

*Our bearer serves tea on the terrace. From left: Jeffrey, Gerd's
Aunt Grete, and me. In the background, the Indus River.*

be something else besides having not enough or a great
deal of money, besides being poor or rich. There must
something else that made life meaningful.

Our life settled into everyday ordinariness. Jeff
played and studied. Gerd sat in his office or drove around
the countryside surveying to determine where pylons
would be placed. One time he came home and told the
story of meeting a very aged farmer who was squatting
by the side of the road. Gerd climbed out of his Jeep and
asked him if this was his land, because he wanted to sur-
vey it. The farmer replied: "No, the land belongs to Allah;
I'm just watching it for Him."

For me this was a noteworthy reply. On the island,
besides ourselves and our servants, lived a *pir*, a Muslim
holy man with a function comparable to that of a priest.

He lived alone in a small temple. We visited him from time to time and brought him fruit or cake. Since we spoke no Urdu, we had to take our chauffeur along as an interpreter. This *pir* gave off a kind of radiance that we could sense clearly. He probably could have told us a great deal, but owing to the unavoidable detour of speaking through the interpreter, who understood nothing of the things we wanted to learn about, no real dialogue could take place. This was a great pity, because it is not often that you encounter a person who you feel could communicate something important to you.

Then Gerd got malaria. I brought him in a mortally ill state to a hospital run by Dutch military doctors. They cared for him and brought him back to health, but it was weeks before he could leave the hospital. During this time, I tried to make myself useful in the hospital. But I must honestly confess that I had to struggle continually with feelings of nausea and revulsion. I am really not suited for hospital work, especially not under the conditions that prevailed in this hospital. Everything that I saw and heard I found extremely discouraging. The setup and equipment were primitive and unhygienic. The doctors did what they could, but there were simply too many patients and too many diseases.

There was another disappointment too. We had taken this job not only because of the money, but also very much because we thought we could help the underprivileged people of this region live an easier life by bringing them electricity. But that turned out to be a Utopian dream. The rich landowners were going to be able to take advantage of it, but the poor people could not in the remotest fashion profit from our innovations. After the power plant was finished, they were in just as miserable a state as before.

Gerd's position of course also involved certain social obligations. We had to relate with colleagues from the Pakistani electric authority, with other engineers who were working on our project or other similar ones, and also with diplomats and consulate functionaries. We often had to take part in receptions in Lahore and Karachi. We would then stay for several days in one of the large luxury hotels.

Functions of this nature always had a rather repellent character for us. Gerd and I arrived at the conviction that we never wanted to live this way. People would come together, do some tongue-wagging, and drink—that was the most important part. On top of it, we were vegetarians, and at these parties there were always mountains of lamb and goat meat prepared in various ways. The table talk interested us not one little bit. We resolved that when the two years were over, we would not renew the contract.

The thing that moved me most deeply in Pakistan were my encounters with the women. In relation to the men, they had not even the most minimal rights, at least not at the time we were there. Perhaps in the meantime a great deal has changed, but I fear very little has. Especially in the country, where we were living, the Pakistani women all wore the *burka*. The *burka* is a garment that covers the women entirely from head to foot. Only small slits for the eyes, covered with lace, make it possible for them to avoid falling flat on their faces when they walk. Only in Karachi did we occasionally see young women without veils.

With Gerd. I'm wearing the burka, *which all women wear when going out so that nothing can be seen of their faces and bodies. Jeffrey is amazed at the sight of his mother.*

Initially I used to go out on the street in my normal clothes, but then I was subjected to having young boys and even older men throw stones at me. A woman who shows her face, our cook explained to me, is deemed a prostitute. It was quite obvious that I was a foreigner, but I was a woman all the same. In order to spare myself such scenes, I finally had a tailor make me a *burka*. It was horribly unpleasant to wear. The worst was, it was very hot under it, and what's more I could see very little. I very seldom went out in it.

In the Koran I read that women are only allowed to show their "private parts" to their husbands. That means, for example, that even a doctor is not allowed to look at them naked. Only in the presence of their husbands is a doctor permitted to grope under the *burka* with his hands in order to examine ailing parts.

Women are supposed to appear in public as little as possible. When Gerd and I would drive together through the countryside, often we would be invited along the way to the houses of landowners or the owners of textile mills. Never was a woman present. If I expressed the wish to do so, I was permitted to visit the women's rooms. On such occasions I heard from the women how unhappy they were. In principle, they were allowed to do nothing but have children and eat. As long as they remained young, they were very beautiful, but since they never moved about, they quickly became shapeless and fat. In the end, eating was their only pleasure.

To such a household belonged a certain young woman from an affluent family who had a good education and spoke English. Her father had been a Pakistani diplomat in the United States. She had married into the family that Gerd and I were visiting. Her marriage had even—very exceptionally—been a love match. She was in a total state of despair about the mode of life that was being imposed on her there. She had founded a school for girls, far and wide the only one. She asked me to visit the school and teach there. But the children couldn't speak English, and I would have been unable to teach it to them quickly enough. Our stay in Pakistan was gradually coming to an end.

I visited the young woman a few times at her school and felt how happy this activity made her. It gave her a sense of self-esteem of which her female in-laws knew nothing. They were profoundly unhappy with the boredom and shut-in quality that were the conditions of their life. Only the old mother-in-law felt everything to be in order. But what had her feelings been when she was young?

Once I invited the women of this house to visit us. They arrived in their black silk *burkas*, which they took off once they were inside. But then our bearer came in with coffee and cakes, and they ran screaming from the room. It was forbidden for him to see their faces! I swore high and low that neither I nor the servant would breathe a mortal word of this. It took a good while for them to calm down and eat the sweet little petits fours the cook had baked especially for them. It was an incredibly big mountain of pastries, quite delicious. They ate every last one.

I asked them if they could not imagine changing their lives. I suggested a few possibilities that I had been thinking about. Oh, they would gladly do that, but how? Not one of them could take any of my ideas seriously or even consider how they might be realized. They were obviously relieved to have been able to speak their minds for once—at the house of a foreigner who wouldn't say anything to anyone else. But the litanies of complaint over their oppressed state did nothing to change the status quo. I am afraid that the women of Pakistan are just as oppressed today as they were thirty-five years ago when I lived there.

I remember very clearly a scene that took place in Sukkur. There were several movie theaters there, and one day a Marilyn Monroe film was advertised. An immense poster was put up showing Marilyn Monroe in a bikini! We happened to pass by and saw hundreds of men standing in front of the poster and staring with open mouths at the movie star's naked flesh. It was quite bizarre. At the same time, their own women were passing by, shrouded entirely in black.

Gerd was quite fond of photography. He held up his camera and took a picture. This move brought him very close to getting beat up; doubtless he would have been if he hadn't run away from there fast as he did. At the least the crowd would have smashed his camera. It was perhaps not right of him to photograph this situation, but the incident showed in a very graphic fashion how unnatural life becomes when one half of the population subjugates the other.

After two years, our contract ran out, but the power plant had still not been built. The project hadn't gone that fast. The plans had been drawn up, accepted, and signed off on. And the camels had carried ten million Canadian dollars' worth of material to the site on their backs. Camels are a sure mode of transport on the desert sands, but they have a will of their own. My experience of them is that they are ill-tempered and nasty. Many of them wore muzzles, for otherwise they would have bitten their owners. And when they didn't want to go, they just lay where they were. We were told that they would only take on loads up to a certain weight. If they were overloaded, they refused to stand up. But it was just this stubbornness that fascinated me about them.

We lived quite near places where the civilization of the Indus valley had flourished five thousand years earlier. Still today, no explanation has been found for its disappearance. An example was Mohenjodara, from which we lived only about forty kilometers distant. People of those ancient times had already had baths in their houses, and there was also an immense public bath. They had paved streets and a system for garbage removal. Around Mohenjodaro lay the fields they cultivated. One of the theories concerning why the city was abandoned by its inhabitants suggests that these fields gradually became infertile and other fields had to be located ever further out into the country. Finally, the people were supposed to have moved to the vicinity of their new fields.

We often visited such abandoned places, of which there were a number in our area. In the sand we found clay beads, jewelry, and beautifully decorated potsherds. Once we discovered a workshop for stone tools and dug up a large number of them. They lay almost on the surface: arrows, arrowheads, hammers, knives. We took a few of them with us and informed the government in Karachi of our find. The museum in Karachi sent a donkey caravan and brought tools by the sackload back to the city. They were five thousand years old and looked exactly like stone tools found in Europe.

Jeff wandered all over our island in the Indus. He found marvelously beautiful things: petrified snails and plants, painted potsherds. We had everything dated by the museum in Karachi. Once he found splendid ceramic tiles. They were from a mosque that had been built on the island in the seventh century. We took a few of these tiles back to Australia.

One day Jeff came home and held both his hands hidden behind his back. "Guess what I've got here, Mommy!" I couldn't guess. It was a small clay horse about ten centimeters long and five centimeters high. And as we found out later, it was a thousand years old!

He still has this little horse. He keeps it in his house in a glass case. It is the only thing he remembers about Pakistan. He has forgotten everything else—the camels, the Indus, the servants, the mornings when I gave him lessons, the cry of the muezzin in the gray dawn light.

As our time on the island reached its end, we packed up all our possessions in boxes and sent them to Australia, where they were stored for us. Gerd had the plan of flying to London, buying a Land Rover caravan, and driving it through Europe, Asia Minor, Kashmir, and India as far as Singapore. From there we would take a ship back to Australia. I am sure that this was Gerd's plan and not mine. However, as always, I let myself be drawn in.

What I was looking for, I had yet to find. So perhaps after all it might be possible to find it in some other place.

Long is the night to one who is wakeful,
Long is a mile to the tired man,
Long is the worldly journey to foolish folk
Who do not know the true Dhamma.
—Dhammapada, verse 60

The Feeling of Freedom

We arrived in London with very little baggage. At the airport we were met by an employee of the Rover firm, who pressed the key of our Land Rover caravan into Gerd's hand. He said, "Have a good trip!" and disappeared. Gerd was not familiar with the vehicle and had never driven in a country where you drive on the left side of the road. You can imagine how interesting the first day of our trip was! Gerd kept looking for the right switches and buttons, while I sat next to him screaming, "Left! Left!" because he kept driving on the wrong side of the road.

Jeffrey sat in the back, completely unperturbed. I cannot remember a single time, during the whole long journey that we already had behind us or during the one that still lay ahead, that this child ever cried, grumbled, or screamed. He always just sat in back and looked out the window. One time we asked him what it was that was so good to look at. He said, "It's just like a movie; everything goes by the window, and I just watch."

We had received letters from my mother and aunts in which they lamented our making the poor child cruise the globe from one end to the other without his ever having any playmates. A child, they reproached us, must have a stable home. Without a doubt, this was an opinion shared by many people. But Jeff seem completely content.

In London we rented a space in a trailer park and set up the interior of the Land Rover for comfortable living. The seats could be folded down to make a double bed. There was a table, a stove; there were cabinets and a sink. The roof of the vehicle could be raised so that you could stand up inside. In the upper area there were two more beds. Jeff slept up there. That felt a little bit like sleeping in a hammock, and he loved it.

We had plenty of time. At our ease, we drove through the charming little English villages to Dover, then through France down to the Côte d'Azur. We weren't expected anywhere and did not have to hold to a fixed itinerary. I remember very vividly the feeling of freedom, of being able to let oneself go with the flow of the days. It was like visiting good friends who wanted to show us their country. Gerd and I had both studied French in school, but the French we knew did not enable us to communicate with the people. Our pronunciation was so bad that no one could understand us, and nobody could or wanted to speak English.

In Monte Carlo I wanted to see what the casino was like so I could add that to my list of experiences. Jeff went to sleep in the Land Rover. We gave the parking lot watchman a tip to keep an eye on our vehicle with the young boy asleep in it. He did his duty, but Jeff didn't stir the whole night, as always. In the casino I was impressed by the elegance of the players and the fact that everything was given away free—drinks, little sandwiches, cigars, cigarettes. But the most interesting thing was watching the people gamble. You saw faces that reflected a greed that people in normal life usually carefully hide. Here it was given free rein. It was an overt, burning greed, and when I saw it, it brought the word "hell" spontaneously to my mind. In German the expression for a gambling den is *Spielhölle*, "gambling hell."

This reminds me of another vivid experience. When I was taking my first course in meditation, already on the second day I had a "hell experience." I had the feeling that I was being held by weird, very thin creatures who looked like stick figures that were dipping me again and again into red-hot tar. As they did this, they kept saying in very high voices: "This is the way to enlightenment. This is the way to enlightenment." I was only able to free myself from them when I stopped meditating. Later I found out that the Buddha had said that once in one's life, one must have a hell experience in order to begin to protect oneself against the dangers of bad karma.

That time in Monte Carlo, I bet two chips at the roulette table. "Rien ne va plus," said the croupier and let go of the ball. Of course I lost—fortunately only a small amount.

We drove on into Spain, and from there to Italy and then Austria. The explanation for this roundabout route is that Gerd did not want to travel in Germany. He said he was not yet able to face it. I myself had long since fully reconciled myself on that score, but he had not been to do this yet. Despite the fact that he continued to speak the German language, he did not want to enter the country in which his family had been murdered. Only recently, just two years ago, he made his peace with Germany, which is very fortunate, for hate and rejection only breed unhappiness—for ourselves and for the entire world.

We visited Vienna and saw the giant Ferris wheel in the Prater. We visited Yugoslavia and saw Dubrovnik, that beautiful city on the sea (at least it was beautiful then). There was folk dancing in colorful traditional dress on the rooftops in the evenings. All the local people and the foreigners would sit together talking on the steps of the steep little lanes, enjoying the music and the lovely dances. We clapped our hands to the rhythm of the music. This is a memory made painful today by the knowledge that in the meantime the city has been nearly destroyed.

Then came Greece and the Acropolis. Once we went to an amphitheater and sat under the open sky watching a classical Greek play being performed in Greek. We didn't understand a word, but that was not important. We sat on those two-thousand-year-old stones, gazed at the actors in their white robes, and listened as though to singing. It was like a fantastic dream.

Then we drove through the Iron Curtain to Bulgaria. With our British and American passports, we had no trouble entering the country. But then it turned out that we couldn't buy anything to eat there. Nothing! The big supermarkets were empty, and of course we had to buy something every day, since we didn't have a refrigerator to keep food. All over, immense posters had been put up that proclaimed that somebody or other had been the best worker last month and had received a medal. But there was not even a dry crust of bread to be found.

Gerd leaned on the gas pedal so we could get to Turkey as fast as possible. We drove along the shore of the Black Sea, and along this beautiful stretch, of all places, we got ourselves into a dangerous situation—the only time during the entire trip.

We had stopped with our caravan in a spot we liked, somewhere out in the midst of nature, as always. We were sitting outside eating our evening meal when suddenly a man with a big knife appeared. He said something; we understood not a word. Maybe he wants something to eat, I thought, and offered him something. But that was not what he wanted. He had a look around, got into the Rover, gave our possessions the once-over, and got out again. The whole time he was waving his knife around. We were beginning to have a very bad feeling about the situation. Then, all of a sudden, he left.

Of course we got out of there; staying would have been too creepy. Gerd drove on till we came to a fruit plantation. There was a watchman there, an old man, who let us drive in through a gate and closed it behind us. He understood a little German. He allowed us to spend the night there and eat as much fruit as we wanted. This helped us to some extent to get over the scare we'd had.

From then on, while we were in Turkey, we parked the Rover in front of a police station every night to sleep. After all, one shouldn't tempt fate.

Maybe we were among the last ones really to travel at their ease in the second half of our century. There was nothing to push us; we didn't have a sightseeing program, the way people do these days. It was a very long journey—like a multicolored carpet, when I look back at it.

In Turkey, we visited Troy, the archaeological site discovered by Schliemann. In Iraq there was unrest at that moment, so we went quickly on to Iran. In Teheran we plunged with our caravan into an inferno of traffic. In those days there was nothing worse than Teheran, as far as traffic was concerned. You got the feeling that utter madmen were on the loose in the streets, and it was obvious nobody was paying the slightest attention to controlling them. But when Gerd made the mistake of turning the wrong way into a one-way street, a policeman appeared instantly. He adopted a stern air and was taking the matter very seriously. We wore him down by speaking Spanish. He didn't understand a word we said. After a half hour, he told us in English that we should drive to the nearest police station. Then he left. Of course we never drove to the police station.

What I remember most of all from Teheran is the markets. Everywhere was the fragrance of spices and oils, and there were gorgeous carpets to be bought. We really had to restrain ourselves to keep from spending our money, which we wanted to use to buy a farm in Australia, before we even got there.

In Afghanistan there was a war going on. We were not even allowed to enter the country. So we drove to Pakistan, where our boxes were waiting for us. No sooner did we arrive in Pakistan than Gerd came down with malaria again. We had to wait a few weeks before he recovered. I had time to visit friends and to have a look at the Indus project, which was slowly progressing. Very slowly—which was no wonder when you consider how the ditches for the foundation walls were being dug: by women in long robes, carrying every shovelful of earth away in little baskets on their heads.

Then we got to India. There we made two quite extraordinary excursions, one to Kashmir and the other to Hunza.

To reach Kashmir, you had to cross the Himalayas on a mountain road. During the trip we got a stunning look at Mount Everest in the morning light. There was snow on the steep road. At one point suddenly there was an Indian army truck coming at us on the wrong side of the road. Gerd couldn't brake because of the snow. We collided. The front of our car was smashed in, but we were able to continue driving. I got a black eye, because when we crashed I was thrown against the windshield. In addition, on this occasion I lost an ivory necklace. Aside from that, nothing bad happened.

When we reached Kashmir, an utterly fabulous job was done fixing the dent in the Rover. The Kashmiris are artists in any handiwork. They produce the most magnificent carvings, fantastic woven goods, embroideries, decorative painting. They are incredibly skilled with their hands. There was no longer the slightest scratch to be seen on our car.

While the Rover was being repaired, we rented a houseboat. I can still clearly see the way it looked. It was furnished almost exclusively with carpets. There were carpets to sit on, carpets on the table, carpets on the walls, carpets on the sleeping benches. And on the carpets were heaps of soft silken cushions. It was very beautiful to look at. And it was wonderfully restorative to have a week's vacation and rest on such a houseboat. Riding in the Land Rover with a little boy who had to be given school lessons every day, for all the freedom, still took a lot out of us.

In Kashmir we became curious about the tomb of Jesus that was supposed to be located not far from the city of Srinagar. We visited it, but were by no means convinced of its authenticity. There are a number of theories—and supposedly proofs—that Jesus had been there and that after his "death" in Jerusalem (which according to this view was only an apparent death) he returned to Kashmir.

Then we were irresistibly attracted by a stony high-mountain area north of Kashmir: Hunza. There in an area of eight thousand square kilometers live roughly ten thousand people who, presumably because of their lifestyle, live to a very old age—a hundred and twenty years and older. "A blithe and happy people," so we had read, with its own language and culture.

To get there, first one has to drive as far as Gilgit, a town on the old caravan route to China. From Gilgit on, everything is uncertain. A single road leads into the country of Hunza—the word "road" being, it must be said, a considerable exaggeration. And "lane" seems far too harmless. "Track of death" would be closer to the fact.

Whatever you call it, this road may only be driven upon by Hunzakuts, inhabitants of Hunza. For anyone else, this is strictly prohibited.

We found a small open army Jeep that was driving up it, which still had three places free. The driver, Jeff, myself, and Gerd, in that order, sat in the front seat. In back, the Jeep was laden down with huge sacks of wheat and oats, and on top of those sat the rest of the passengers, six Hunzakuts. The road was exactly the width of the Jeep and very steep. It went along a cliff face. So on the right was the wall, on the left the drop down to the Hunza River. There were hairpin curves so narrow that even the turning radius of the little Jeep wasn't small enough to negotiate them in one go. This vehicle itself was not exactly in the best of shape. It seems to have been cobbled together out of parts from other Jeeps that had presumably been left behind by various expeditions.

Just before we began the trip up, our driver stopped at a little temple, prayed there for a few minutes, and then tossed a coin into a bowl. He had done that, he told us, so that we wouldn't fall off the road into the river. Since I was obviously looking at him somewhat oddly, he added that this was a frequent occurrence. Recently, a small bus had fallen and thirty people had been killed. At that point I gave him another coin to put in the bowl.

I must quite honestly say that at this stage, I had not begun to come to terms with my own death. I still urgently wanted to remain alive. Today it's different, but at that time, the idea of disappearing from the face of the earth was not something I took for granted or found consoling. In addition, my thoughts went to Jeffrey and Irene, whom I wanted to see again.

In any case, we continued on our way, and against all expectations, everything went fine. Once we came to a place where the road had been destroyed. A few Hunzakuts were there repairing it. We had to wait until they were finished. Then we were able to go on.

At last we reached the first Hunzakut village. Our driver had a large number of relatives and friends in this town, who greeted him joyously. He was invited to go have a drink. I asked him what he drank. He drank Hunzapani. *Pani* means "water," but Hunzapani is not water but wine, to which our driver proceeded to help himself, liberally.

A few of our fellow riders climbed out and a few sacks were unloaded. This was repeated a couple of times more, and then we and the driver were alone. He was clearly in a state of good cheer and sang as he drove. The road hadn't altered in the least. It was still just as steep and curvy as before. I was getting an increasingly bad feeling about the whole thing.

By good fortune, we arrived in one piece in Baltit, the capital, which lay at an altitude of three and a half thousand meters. There was an inn in which we could rent a room. It was a quite primitive place, but it had an incredibly beautiful view. It is impossible to imagine the beauty of that place. Before us was a panorama of the entire Himalayan range. The sun coming up in the morning in this setting was one of nature's indescribable shows.

No sooner had we arrived than a messenger from the *mir* appeared. The *mir* of Hunza is, in effect, the king of the country. Politically, Hunza is part of Pakistan, but it is administered autonomously. The messenger informed us that we should come for a meal the following day. We were quite pleased. We were total strangers and had just arrived, and we had received an invitation from the *mir*! We spiffed ourselves up and went.

The *mir* lived in a handsome wooden chalet rather than a true palace. His residence was what we could call a lovely wooden house with many splendid carvings on

In Hunza. All Hunzakuts wear the same hats. In the middle is Sultan Ali, cousin of the Mir, *director of the postal service, school principal, and tourist guide.*

the façade. We went in, and there he sat with his *rani*, the queen. She had quite fair skin and was pretty as a picture. He had had seven children with her, as he immediately told us. We estimated that he himself was around fifty, which in Hunza made him a young man.

The first thing he asked was how we had managed to get there. Well, with a Jeep, we said. But he was referring to something else. Entry into the country was prohibited. For a long time, no tourists had come. The background of his question was as follows. Hunza lies on the Tibetan border, and at that time the Chinese had invaded Tibet. They had sealed the borders even of the small bordering countries. No one was allowed either in or out.

We had gotten a permit for the journey in Karachi. In his opinion, we had surely received it by error. He was happy to see us. It had been forever since he had been with people he could talk to. He spoke perfect English; he frequently traveled to Europe to go to the Côte d'Azur. He was a friend of Prince Rainier of Monaco and missed very much having suitable company.

The second part of our conversation revolved around a quite concrete question: whether we knew anything about kerosene refrigerators. Gerd said, "Yes, as it happens, we know something about them." We had made use of just such an apparatus in our house on the island in Pakistan. The *mir* indicated that he had just gotten a new one. It had been carried up to Baltit by several Hunzakuts, who had taken turns carrying it on their backs. And now nobody could get it to work.

On hearing this, Gerd went into the kitchen and did what we always had done when our own refrigerator went on strike. He turned it upside down. It had to stay that way overnight, Gerd explained. Tomorrow morning we would come back and by then it would be working fine.

We came back the next morning, Gerd turned the refrigerator over, and in fact it worked. Of course from then on we enjoyed the high esteem of the *mir*. He asked Gerd if he didn't want to stay and set up electricity in the country. This did not fit with our plans, however. We gave the *mir* to understand that we were obliged to decline his offer. On the other hand, we were of course quite happy to accept his invitation for lunch.

At the table were the *mir*, the *rani*, two of their daughters, and ourselves. Before each of us was a small glass bowl containing rose petals. Jeffrey inspected his own little bowl, picked it up, and drank it dry. I whispered to him, "That's not to drink, that's to wash your fingers in." So it was in Hunza of all places that he became acquainted with fine table manners.

I looked with admiration at the magnificent silver, which was decorated with a crown and a monogram. I asked the *mir* if it was a family heirloom. No, he told me, he had just had it made recently. Up till a short time ago, everyone here had eaten with their fingers.

I remember every detail of this luncheon. There were fourteen courses. First there was a venison rib roast, then fish, then chicken, then goose, and then a number of other things I was unable to identify. Everything was delicious, and behind each chair was a servant who served his particular diner. I asked how the *mir* was able to acquire all these delicacies way up here. He told me they were brought to him by the inhabitants of Hunza. Instead of paying taxes, they brought him a part of whatever they grew in their fields or raised in their barns. In addition he received a government salary from Pakistan. In exchange for that, he saw to it that wheat and oats were stockpiled in barns for next year's sowing or in case of famine, Allah forbid.

The *mir* of Hunza was a vassal of the Aga Khan, the religious leader of a Muslim sect. The *mir* was his representative in all questions of religion.

But the real reason we had traveled to Hunza was on account of the longevity the people enjoyed there. We wanted to know how the people lived that made it possible for them to reach such elevated ages and still remain healthy. We were particularly interested in how they ate. Nutrition had been an object of study for us since we lived on the ranch in Mexico.

It turned out that there were two things that were responsible for the longevity and health of the people there. First of all was the fact that they lived at three and a half thousand meters' altitude in thin air and had to breathe deeply when they were walking anywhere on their stony paths. The whole of Hunza is a pedestrian zone, with exception made only for the Jeep that comes once a week. The second factor was that very good apricots grew up there. The people dried them and ate them throughout the year. From the pits they made an apricot oil that they used for cooking, rubbed in their hair, and spread on bread.

Apart from that, their diet was rather lopsided. They could hardly ever afford meat. They ate wheat or rice and a few vegetables. Without the apricots, the vitamin and mineral content of their diet would surely have been deficient. Perhaps the tough constitutions of the Hunzakuts came from the water they drank. I must give an account of our own experience with this water.

Once a month, the *mir* took his seat in a hall that was open on all sides and covered by a beautiful roof that rested on marvelously carved pillars. There he dispensed the law. Anyone who had a complaint about anything could come there, and the *mir* would decide cases in dispute. His word was law and was followed without question. We were once present at such a court proceeding. It took place just as it must have many hundreds of years ago.

The *mir* told us that most of the disputes were related to the irrigation of the postage-stamp-size fields that lay on the steep slopes. Glacier water was channeled into little canals, and each farmer was allowed to let it flow onto his fields in turn. There were always claims that someone had taken too much of the water by letting it flow onto his field too long rather than sticking to the prescribed time.

It became the established custom for us to eat at the *mir*'s, for Gerd to look after the kerosene refrigerator, and for Jeff to play with the *mir*'s two little daughters. One day Jeff got sick. This time it was really something serious. It was doubtless due to his inability to tolerate the water from the glaciers, which was very high in mineral content and quite milky by the time it arrived in the cisterns. The locals also called it "glacier milk."

Jeff had a high fever and could neither eat nor drink. He was really in a bad way. We had to get back down to a doctor as quickly as possible. Up there, there weren't any. When we said goodbye to the *mir* and his family, he handed us a gold Rolex watch. Every day, he said, it lost half a minute. Would we please give it to the Rolex company in Switzerland, have it properly adjusted, and then brought to the Aga Khan in Gstaad. The Aga Khan would give it back to the *mir* the next chance he got.

We didn't want to say no, so we took the costly thing with us and hid it in our toolbox. After all, we were not set up to transport such objects of value.

We later sent the watch to Rolex in Switzerland as a piece of sealed registered mail with an accompanying letter. It did in fact arrive there. In what manner the *mir* might have gotten it back, I do not know. I don't even know if he is still alive. If he has reached the typical age of Hunzakuts, it is quite possible that he is.

As a last token of his friendship, the *mir* put his Jeep and personal driver at our disposal to get us back to Gilgit. Of course his driver drove very well and there were no sacks loaded on with us and no extra Hunzakuts. He also didn't drink any Hunzapani, so the drive was no problem for him. Thus the trip back was far more pleasant than our trip up to Baltit had been. Only I was very nervous, because my boy was so sick. Jeff didn't make a single sound the whole way.

Down in Gilgit, we caught a plane to Lahore. We had sent a telegram ahead to an electrical engineer who had worked with Gerd on the Indus project. We told him that we were in immediate need of an apartment and a doctor. When we arrived, both needs were already being taken care of. It turned out that Jeff had a liver infection. A few days later, Gerd had a malaria relapse. Whenever we were in Pakistan, he came down with this disease, never anywhere else.

I put the two of them in two different rooms so that they wouldn't infect each other and took care of them. After about two weeks they were both pretty much back on their feet.

I never got sick on our journeys. I didn't have time. I was much too busy making sure all three of us survived.

Our Rover caravan was waiting for us in Lahore. The city is on the border between Pakistan and India. We crossed the border there.

The first thing we saw in India was the big golden temple of the Sikhs in Amritsar. It stands in the middle of a lake. It is a fantastic sight, which could make a person forget how much unrest there is in this area. We visited the temple and listened to the chanting. The Sikhs are a Hindu sect and generally peaceful. That two Sikhs killed the daughter of Nehru is incomprehensible to me.

We drove to New Delhi and to Jaipur, and to Ahmedabad, where there are caves with Buddhist frescoes roughly one thousand years old in them. We went to Bombay, where to begin with we cooled off at the Hilton Hotel. As a foreigner, one could go into any of the hotels and simply sit down in the air-conditioned lobby and relax in the cool air.

In Bangalore we were invited by a judicial official to visit his house. I had a great desire at last to take a bath again. He took me to the bathroom, where there was a huge barrel full of hot water. I got in and nearly got myself cooked. I had gone about the thing entirely the wrong way. What you do is first soap yourself; then you take a big ladle and, standing in front of the barrel, you pour the hot water over your head. So it's really a kind of shower.

In South India we went to Tiruvannamalai in the vicinity of Madras. This is a famous place where one of India's greatest enlightened sages lived, a *rishi* named Ramana Maharshi. He died in 1950, so we didn't meet him personally, but we went to his ashram and learned something about him and his teaching from an Englishman, Arthur Osborne, who had lived with him for twenty-five years. An ashram is a place where people who wish to train in the teaching of a particular sage live, eat, receive teaching, and read and study together.

Ramana Maharshi repeatedly stressed that the condition of attaining enlightenment was getting rid of the illusion of ego. One should investigate by asking oneself,

S H A M B H A L A

SHAMBHALA

If you wish to receive a copy of the latest Shambhala Publications catalogue of books and to be placed on our mailing list, please send us this card — or send us an e-mail at info@shambhala.com

Please print

BOOK IN WHICH THIS CARD WAS FOUND ....

NAME ....

ADDRESS ....

CITY .... STATE ....

ZIP OR POSTAL CODE ....

COUNTRY (*if outside U.S.A.*) ....

Detach bookmark before mailing card.

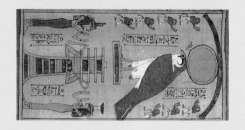

"Who am I?" For Gerd, what was communicated here was very important. To this day, he goes to this ashram every year. For me it was different. At that time, I was not in a position to investigate who I was. I had no idea what means could be used to do that. And Ramana Maharshi had not given instructions for this.

We lived in the ashram and also ate there, off huge banana leaves that served as plates, and with our hands. Jeff was especially fond of that. I thought to myself, this is all quite wonderful, and Ramana Maharshi was doubtless a great and wise man. But I didn't know how I could apply his wisdom to myself. I longed for concrete instructions, for a clear plan of action. Then all of a sudden I had the feeling that I was near the object of my longing, at the beginning of my spiritual path.

Just like a deep lake,
Crystal-clear and undisturbed—
So the wise also become clear
Once they have heard the Dhamma.
—Dhammapada, verse 82

The Beginning of My Own Path

From Ramana Maharshi's ashram, we drove on to the city of Pondicherry, which had formerly been a French colony. This is where the Sri Aurobindo ashram was. We had heard of Sri Aurobindo, a great sage who had lived here. At the time we were there, he was already dead. A woman was leading the ashram, a Frenchwoman who had been his companion and was known by all as "the Mother."

The Sri Aurobindo ashram was immense, almost as big as the whole city. Everywhere were houses in which activities were going on that served to propagate Sri Aurobindo's teaching. We rented a room in the ashram.

The Indians considered the Mother to be a holy woman—which, by the way, in India is something that comes about more easily than elsewhere. The people have a great need to venerate saints. Regardless of that, the Mother was definitely a very special person.

A kind of friendship grew up between the Mother and Jeffrey. He went to see her every day, which was something quite unusual for him. She kept herself very secluded. Visitors had to be announced. Yet he climbed up the steps to where she lived every day to have a talk with her. It must have been enjoyable for her. She herself had children. One of her sons was an architect and had designed one of the buildings at the ashram.

The teachings of Sri Aurobindo struck me as far too complicated. By contrast, what the Mother taught was very simple and very straightforward. I had a sense of connection with it. She also taught meditation.

There was a very interesting school there, interesting enough so that we were considering sending Jeffrey there. It was a school in which spiritual things were taught. But Jeffrey didn't want to go there and didn't want to be separated from his parents.

This school had a big schoolyard. We used to gather there in the evenings under the stars. During the day, it was so hot that it was almost intolerable. This was April, the hottest month. But in the evenings it was lovely—cool with a clear starry sky. Over the loudspeaker the Mother would give instructions for meditation, which I would follow. I felt immediately that this was the right thing for me. The instructions were very similar to those given by the Buddha.

From that time on, I have been meditating. That is now thirty-four years ago. I immediately had the feeling that this was the path I had been looking for. Now I could turn inward.

The Mother gave very good, realistic, clear, lucid, and simple instructions for living a harmonious life. Later she was to found an international village, Auroville, where people from all over the world who wanted to lead a spiritual life gathered. I can only look back on the Mother with great gratitude. We spent a few months with her. For me, this was the gateway to the path of spiritual growth. The clear instructions and simple words she used showed me what had to be done.

Not that the words Ramana Maharshi had used were unclear. (In fact, he never wrote anything: what he said was written down later.) But he spoke from the vantage point of enlightenment, and for me that was a step too far, a number too large. By contrast, the Mother spoke about the things we are in contact with every day.

After our stay at Sri Aurobindo Ashram, we drove around in India some more. Two experiences stick especially vividly in my memory.

We were in Calcutta. We had parked our caravan in the courtyard of the Automobile Club to pass the night. There was a man sitting on the street, right on the corner, selling oranges. I said to Jeff, "Here's five rupees. Go and buy a bag of oranges." He went and never came back.

It got later and later. Both Gerd and I went out to look for him. Maybe Jeff had misunderstood me and had gone to the market. It started to get dark. This was a repetition of the nightmare of Iquitos. But in Calcutta we had the additional worry that children here were kidnapped and then—very often after having been mutilated—trained as beggars and made to live as part of beggar families. Such were the rumors; I don't know if they were true or not. In any case, we were terribly frightened.

When we were unable to find him, we went back to the Automobile Club and announced that a boy was lost. The Club immediately mobilized all its motorcyclists, who decided to comb the city and were just about to set out when Jeff nonchalantly came around the corner with a bag of oranges in his hand.

We were all over him. "For heaven's sake, where were you?" Jeff responded by telling the following story. As he was buying the oranges, a man with a cow came by. He would milk this cow on the street, then ring the nearest doorbell. He would sell the housewife the freshly drawn milk in a pitcher. She would pour out the milk in the house and then bring the pitcher back. And Jeff had tagged along with the man and watched. After a while he had asked the man if he could perhaps help him. Yes, of course, the man had said.

Jeff went with the man and the cow from house to house. First he was allowed to hold the cow. Then he was allowed to do some of the milking. Then he was allowed to bring the milk to the housewife. And that four hours had passed while all this was going on, he never noticed at all.

On this occasion, I decided that one way or another I was going to do away with my constant pursuit of the child in my thoughts as well as my ongoing fear for his life. Because these things made it impossible for me to take joy in his life. Every mother, whether of a small child or of grown children, knows this. You are in a constant state of worry.

I wanted to get rid of this fetter. Meditation, I felt,

Jeffrey and I having lunch in Singapore. Street vendors sell good, cheap food.

was the way to do it. I realized that it was not possible to dissolve it all at once. But one day I would be capable of doing so. So that the reader does not misunderstand me: I loved my children and I still do. However, my attachment and my fear can only have a negative influence on my love. My children do not belong to me; they belong to themselves. I'm not their keeper, any more than they are my keepers. We are linked to each other, but not bound to each other—that is a huge difference.

My experiences during our extended journey helped me a great deal to undertake an inner journey as well. If I hadn't made that trip with Jeff and Gerd, it would have been much more difficult for me to attain clarity about myself. I would have stayed in my pretty little house in San Diego, fulfilled my daily responsibilities, and presumably not have changed in any important way between my thirty-fifth year and my seventieth. I would never have encountered my limits and been able to go beyond them.

The second experience that is connected in my memory with India was a meeting in a park where we had stopped to spend the night. I was sitting in front of our car looking off into the distance, and there I saw a white-clad swami, an Indian Hindu monk. He had a black braid hanging from the back of his head. I looked at him and said to Gerd, "You know what? That's a European!" Europeans walk entirely differently from Indians, and they also have a different sort of physical build. I said, "Go ahead over and invite him for a cup of tea." Gerd went after him and made the invitation.

He was an Australian, and his swami name was Narikutti. He was happy to join us in the caravan. We could serve tea there, because we had a little stove. Narikutti accompanied us for a leg of our journey. He taught us about Hindu mythology, basing his expositions on the temples we visited, in which many of the gods were painted on the walls or depicted in sculptures. South India had magnificent temples, where very often there was an elephant in residence. We learned the name and significance of gods like Shiva, Ganesha, and Hanuman, but I must honestly say that the worship of gods was not my way. I found the stories interesting, and they were a gateway for me to an understanding of the Hindu way of thinking—but that's all.

Narikutti also came with us to Sri Lanka. Then he went back and spent the rest of his life in a cave that had had an addition built onto it, on the slopes of Mount Arunachala, next to Ramana Maharshi's ashram. He is now long dead, though he was only three or four years older than I. We corresponded with him for a few years after that. I count him as one of our teachers. There were three people to whom we owe a lot, since they made it possible for us to embark on the path: Ramana Maharshi, the Mother, and Narikutti.

We remained in India for about a year. In those days, in the sixties, there were very few foreign tourists, and when you met one, you immediately struck up a friendship. We were able to provide practical help to a number of them, because we had medicines with us.

From India we took a ferry to Sri Lanka and traveled throughout the country. We saw it as a paradise. It was completely peaceful, everywhere people smiled at us and gave us coconuts and bananas; and we could bathe in the sea and see the most beautiful, brightly colored fish. There we had our first contact with Buddhism. Later I would found a convent in Sri Lanka, but this was still a long way off.

From there we took a ship to Thailand—ever nearer to Buddhism, or so it seems to me in retrospect.

What we felt the most in Bangkok and other Thai cities was admiration and wonder. The sight of the peaceful Buddha statues, the golden ornaments, the emerald Buddha carved from a single large gemstone—all this was simply overwhelming. With all the marvelous temple complexes, we couldn't stop looking. We got to know a few Thai monks who spoke English and whom we could ask about their religion. What they explained to us was more or less just the ritual and not what really mattered to me, which was simply how to live one's life.

From Thailand our way took us to Cambodia. We

borrowed bicycles and in this way made a thorough tour of Angkor Wat, where we visited the glorious temples long ago built by the Khmer people and accidentally rediscovered by archaeologists. We were almost alone as we moved about within the temple complexes. The stillness and sacredness of the place, with its numerous Buddha heads, stone sculptures of divine female dancers, and devas (higher beings like angels) made a tremendous impression on us.

Before their rediscovery, the buildings and figures were completely overgrown by jungle. Fig trees had pushed their roots into every crack. In some spots the jungle and buildings were left just as they had been found. Beneath the dense foliage and convoluted tangle of branches and roots, one saw the ancient stones—and over everything was a great stillness.

From Pnom Penh, the capital, we took another memory with us. There was a bird market there, where birds were sold out of cages to people who then immediately set them free in order to create good karma. Directly then, the bird dealers would recapture the birds and put them on sale again. We found this very strange indeed, and it made Jeff cry.

Our next destination was Vietnam. At first sight, Saigon seemed quite beautiful and untouched by the war that had already broken out heavily further to the south. But one was reminded of it by the many foreign journalists sitting around in the hotels. Thus Saigon was no longer an entirely pleasant place to be. Thus we decided it would be best to get on a ship and head for our destination, Singapore. In Singapore we sold our valiant Land

Rover and booked passage on a freighter that would take us to Freemantle, Australia.

It was a Danish freighter, on which there was really only room for twelve passengers. But Jeff was allowed to come on board as the thirteenth passenger. He was given his own cabin, which he thought was just wonderful. We were assigned the shipowner's cabin, which was composed of a sitting room, a bedroom, and a bathroom. The cook even provided us with vegetarian cuisine—and that on a ship whose cargo was frozen meat.

We stopped everywhere along the way, including Indonesia and Timor. We were able to go ashore and get a look at the ports and the areas around them. In Darwin, the northernmost port in Australia, we stopped for a week. It was a very comfortable and restful, slowpoke voyage.

Finally we arrived at Freemantle. Freemantle is the port of Perth. We disembarked. It was August, and in Australia that's winter. A little befuddled, we stood in the cold and froze. From Perth we traveled to Sydney, where we looked for and found our Jeep and our boxes and settled everything with the authorities. Then we cruised in the Jeep to Queensland on the east coast, the place we had liked the best five years earlier.

Near Brisbane, the capital of Queensland, we bought a farm. The climate there is very pleasant.

The farm was about two hundred Australian acres, which is about seventy-two hectares. The landscape was one of hills, valleys, and meadows and there was a large primeval rainforest, in which wild orchids, lianas, and palms grew. The farm also had a small pond in which we could swim and cool off.

On the farm was a house with electricity and telephone, with a tumbledown garage and a barn. The whole thing had become the property of a bank after the original owners had simply disappeared. They had gone bankrupt. The bank asked us for three thousand pounds. We offered two thousand pounds, which they were more than happy to take. Today that's something like $2,700—for two hundred acres of land and a house!

It was a wonderful piece of the earth. We had nothing but nice neighbors on the nearby farms, and they were a great help to us at the beginning. After all, we were both city children and were not very familiar with agriculture.

The farmers around us were primarily dairy farmers. We began to consider how we might be able to use the meadows in a different way. One way or the other, the grass would have to be used to feed animals. However, we didn't want to raise animals that would have to be slaughtered. So we decided to raise Shetland ponies—nobody kills Shetland ponies. Our idea was to sell the young animals to the parents of children who wanted ponies.

"I had a farm in Africa." This is the way a famous novel by Isak Dinesen begins. Gerd and I had a farm in Australia. Ours was the first organic farm in the region. We cultivated organic whole foods, without a single spray of insecticide or other poison. That was a lot of work. We were able to grow so much for our own sustenance that we only had to spend about a hundred dollars a year for food. For that, we bought rice, raisins, and brown sugar. Often we were able to barter our excess fruit for other things we needed.

Gradually our organic farm became known, because

*With a young
Shetland pony.*

Gerd also wrote some articles about it. Young people showed up and looked the place over.

Gerd was (and still is today) very active. On our property he planted five hundred fruit trees of different kinds; in addition he planted spruce and eucalyptus trees. Altogether there were twenty thousand saplings, which were intended one day to bring us an income.

Our Shetland ponies were totally charming. There is nothing cuter than a newborn Shetland pony, which looks like a big poodle.

We also had horses for riding. Jeffrey's favorite horse to ride around the farm was a well-behaved old mare named Flicka. He can remember her: at that time he was about twelve years old. Flicka was so good-natured that you could do anything with her at all. But one time she was spooked by something. A leaf fell or something else like that happened. She stopped in mid-gallop, and Jeff crashed to the ground. I was standing at the window watching. He remained lying on his back without moving. At this moment I had the thought: he's dead. And at the same moment I felt within me the capacity to accept the life or death of my child, whichever it happened to be. A minute later, he came out of it and began to yell; then I knew he was alive. He had come down hard on his back and the wind had momentarily been knocked out of him.

For me that was the first actual gesture of letting go of my children. For the first time I could regard Jeffrey and Irene (who was still living in San Diego) as people I loved but who were not an inseparable part of me. This in no way signified cutting off my love for them, quite the contrary. I became capable of loving them without fear, right from the heart, without that love being conditional on any requirement or demand. My love for them did not depend on their being alive; on their living the way I wanted them to; on, from their side, their feeling connected to me, on their being grateful to me, or on their being "well-behaved." All that no longer mattered.

The Buddha had a son named Rahula. Rahula means "fetter." He gave him this name when he was born, because he knew a child is a fetter on the heart.

I had already had two similar experiences with Jeffrey, in Iquitos and in Calcutta. And a by no means small factor was the fact that I had had to leave Irene behind at home, because she did not want to go on the journey with us. That was not at all easy for me. It often tormented me not to have her near me.

It took a long time before I could say: They're there, they're my children; I love them very much, but I could also cope with their death. Without this letting go, it is impossible to experience a pure love. It is true one can still love, but always with the fear of loss. It was not easy to get rid of that fear, but on the day that Flicka threw Jeff to the ground, I succeeded in doing it.

Health is the greatest wealth,
Contentment the most beautiful treasure,
Confidence is the best of friends,
Nirvana the supreme happiness.
—Dhammapada, verse 204

From the Farm to the Beginnings of Monastic Life

On our farm we had a little milk house. It was beneath some big trees, and it was always cool inside. In little milk houses like this, the dairy farmers of the area used to keep their milk until it was picked up. In the old days, there were no refrigerators. Our little milk house was empty, because we didn't produce any milk. We made it into a little temple, a temple to all religions, because we were not yet in agreement about which religion we wanted to follow.

We had brought back souvenirs from all the countries we had visited during our many journeys. They now found a place in this temple—from Hindu gods to Buddha statues to religious carvings of the aborigines. Our archaeological finds were also represented, as well as articles of Jewish worship, candleholders and lamps.

Our farm was called Shalom, an Israeli greeting meaning "peace." It was really meant to be a place of peace. We meditated in our little milk house every day.

There was an enormous amount of work to do on the farm. I was constantly busy turning over soil, pulling out weeds, carrying away stones.

I was frequently in fear for our lives, our survival. The worst experience at Shalom was a forest fire, which one day came over the hill into our valley. Only someone who has tried to fight fire without water can imagine the exhaustion and fear that comes over people in such circumstances. More than a hundred neighbors came to our aid, to save our house, our trees, and our animals. The goats and horses were locked up in the house, and the house was watched by the volunteer fire department. But the trees and the meadows were saved by our neighbors with shovels, sacks, and lots of farmer's wisdom.

The women brought drinks and bread, and climbed up the hills to take them to the men. After six hours of fear, uncertainty, exhaustion, smoke clouds, and suffocating heat, the worst was over. After that we had to hold a "fire watch" for two days, for in the heat of Australia, hot wood is easily reignited.

In Australia the weather is very extreme. Rain is simply called a storm. And indeed, every rainfall quickly works itself up into a storm. At least once a year, Queensland is struck by typhoons so powerful that they rip the roofs off houses. Our roof was never blown off, but I did experience having huge tree trunks, carried by rainwater from the surrounding hills, dashed through our garden as if by sea breakers.

At the beginning, these storms made me panic. Of course, I eventually got used to them, but at the beginning I felt completely vulnerable. Our farm was rather isolated. The closest neighbor was more than a kilometer away. As a city child, I was not familiar with this raging of the elements. It gave me quite a scare.

Also the many poisonous snakes found in Australia upset me considerably. It was quite a long time before I was able to accept them as a normal and natural part of life on the farm.

Sometimes my thoughts went back to the house in San Diego, to my existence as a housewife, to that totally normal life. Although I never had the wish to be back there, our travels, on which we exposed ourselves without protection to to danger, to the alien and the unknown, did demand a considerable adjustment from me. Now, in retrospect, I can acknowledge that in the course of those travels I had to face a great deal of fear. But I always believed that it is only possible to overcome fear by doing, in spite of the fear, the very thing that triggers it. And if one fails to do this, one never gets to know one's own strengths, which on the spiritual level are unlimited.

I have learned to find certainty within myself no matter where I am. And I have learned that people, no matter how they look and no matter what language they speak, are the same everywhere. All of them want to be happy, and none of them are. It was not possible to miss seeing that.

Life is a long process of letting go. That is something I understood at that time. I don't believe that without my travels I would have been able to complete this process. I don't believe that I would have been able to live on the farm if I'd gone straight there from San Diego.

On Shalom we had chickens, a pair of peafowl, seven goats, two riding horses, cats, dogs, and twenty-five Shetland ponies. In the way we ate, we lived up to the advice of the health books in every respect. Thus we drank no coffee, no black tea—only infusions made from herbs and leaves we had dried ourselves. We ate very little sugar. Instead of that, we had honey from our own bees. We had milk and butter from our own goats, fruits and vegetables we had grown ourselves, bananas from our banana plantation, and grains free from insecticides and other poisons.

In spite of all this, I got pernicious anemia. At first, I had no idea what was the matter with me. I felt completely limp, so tired and drained of energy that I could hardly walk up the stairs. The doctor whom I eventually consulted saw immediately that I was far too pale. He diagnosed pernicious anemia and explained to me that this was a disease one never got rid of one's whole life long. As long as one lived, one had to get vitamin B_{12} shots.

I was not at all pleased by this prospect. I was still young and did not fancy the idea of being a perpetual patient. I took matters into my own hands and embarked on a three-month fast with grape juice. That meant nothing but juice and, several times a day, some dark grapes. I'd read about it in a book.

This cure worked extremely well. When I was finished with it, my blood levels were right again and have remained so to this day. After the cancer operation I had three years ago, they temporarily went out of balance, but then too, I got them back to normal. I live now as I did then, as simply and naturally as possible, only abstaining from meat, which is not difficult for me.

One day we were visited on the farm by a Buddhist monk. He was an Englishman called Phra Khantipalo. He had no home, and so we invited him to live with us. We temporarily gave him our guest room, while he and Gerd built a wooden hut, or *kuti,* for him in the middle of the woods on our property. He lived with us and ate with us, and we learned a great deal from him.

As Phra Khantipalo was telling us about the Buddha's teaching, something became clear to me: I could understand and practice this. Take for example the doctrine of the five virtues. One may not kill any living being; take what is not given; lie or use coarse language; engage in any sexual misconduct; take drugs or drink alcohol. One should practice the opposites of these: loving-kindness, generosity, reliability and loyalty, right speech, and mindfulness.

This was the first time I had heard something of which I could say: I understand this completely, I don't have to think about it at all. I know that it's right, I know what I have to try to achieve. Here was a spiritual path that really showed how you can change in order to attain inner purity. I organized courses on our farm, which the monk gave for interested people. I also invited other teachers.

Both of us continued to study with Phra Khantipalo. For me it was a fulfilling experience to know at last where I was headed. This became my ruling idea. It became clear to me that though our healthy, natural life was indeed

My first meditation course with Phra Khantipalo. I am seated on the ground, third from the right. Phra Khantipalo is standing behind me.

helpful, it did not provide the happiness and peace I was seeking.

Meanwhile Jeffrey had reached the age of eighteen and had moved to Brisbane, the capital, in order to attend the university there. He really wanted to become an electrical engineer like Gerd, but after two years he switched to computer science. Since he had done exceptionally well in school, the government paid both his tuition and living costs.

One day I flew to America and visited the Zen Center in San Francisco. From there I went to Tassajara, a magnificent place in a valley on the other side of the Carmel mountains on the coast of California. It has hot springs and a big mountain lake. I stayed there for three months so I could learn about Zen Buddhism too.

It was a wonderful time. I was on the staff there, so I didn't have to pay for anything. My job was to keep the bathhouse clean. Thus I was able to jump into the hot springs as often as I wanted to. But I missed the teaching of the Buddha as it had been taught by Phra Khantipalo.

Zen Buddhism follows the teaching discourses of the Zen masters down through the centuries. Zen came to China in the sixth century (as Ch'an) and later, in the twelfth century, to Japan, and it developed in a way that was appropriate to Chinese and Japanese culture. Exactly the same thing happened with Tibetan Buddhism, which developed in close conjunction with Tibetan culture.

The Theravada Buddhism that I follow today follows the original 2,500-year-old teaching of the Buddha. We hope to get this teaching to take root here in the West so that it becomes native and normalized here too. It could contribute to the enrichment of religious life in Europe, without suppressing the existing teachings.

When I returned to Australia, I had the feeling that Gerd had disapproved of my absence. We were together again, and I had a lot to tell him. After all, he was also very interested in Buddhism. I was sure that he wished the best for me on my path. It was not clear to me at this time that his interest was neither as urgent nor as deep-seated as mine. Later it came out that he saw in my absence and new independence a rejection of his ideals of organic agriculture. But initially I noticed nothing of this nature.

Our farm, our little milk house, and the *kuti* in the woods attracted other teachers. They came, gave talks, and taught yet other methods of meditation.

I flew to Burma. In those days, you could only stay

in the country for seven days. Then you had to leave the country and could come back with a new visa. I repeated that process three times. Three times seven days I meditated at a center under the guidance of students of U Bha Khin, who was not a monk but a layman. U Bha Khin was the finance minister of Burma, and in his ministry it was the policy that people could only be employed there who had done a meditation course with him. To my knowledge, as a result of this approach, the finance ministry functioned particularly well.

From Burma I returned home. But from this time onward, I increasingly spent more time away. I attended meditation courses and organized a few of them; and at some point one of my teachers told me I myself could give a course on our farm. We had enlarged the garage, and a larger number of participants could now meditate there.

I had April in mind as the time when Gerd and I could give a course. Gerd wrote out the invitations. He had already indicated his willingness to practice yoga with the participants.

Four weeks prior to that, I went to southern Australia to do a meditation course. When I came back home, Jeffrey was waiting at the railway station. I asked, "Where's Daddy?" He said, "Here's a letter."

And then I thought to myself, what I'm seeing is not real. In the letter Gerd wrote that he had left. He wrote that he believed I would be better able to develop in my new world if he was no longer there.

Today I realize that he was right. I had always thought we could travel this path together, and we did go a fair distance on it together. But he was not able to devote himself to the spiritual path with the same all-out steadiness as I could. At that time I was horrified and also furious. For there I now was: with a huge farm, twenty-five horses, lots of machines—all our goods and possessions. Gerd took nothing with him. He just left with his backpack.

Maybe life on the farm was also too sedentary for him. We had built up the whole place, worked ourselves to the bone, and now the whole thing was working and in good order. Nothing further had to be changed; nothing new had to be undertaken. Maybe that was another reason he had lost interest in the place. He had then, and still has today, the nature of a pioneer. We had lived on the farm for fourteen years.

While I was still standing on the train platform with the letter in my hand, it was already clear to me that I would not be able to run the farm by myself. And in practice that was quickly confirmed. To begin with, I couldn't deal with the machines. For instance, I couldn't repair the pump that pumped water from the spring to the house.

Jeffrey was in Brisbane at the university. He came home on weekends and helped me, but of course he was also unaccustomed to this work and it was very difficult for him.

I tried to sell the farm. That was not an easy thing at this time. Land was not selling just then because there was a crisis in the economy. People had no money.

First I sold the horses. Fortunately I was able to get rid of them all. But the horses had to be loaded for transport, and this was something you had to know how to do. I had an idea of how to do it, but only a theoretical one. Gerd had always taken care of this. The result was that once while I doing it, I got a terrible kick from one of the horses. In fact it's not an easy thing to transport horses in a trailer.

Then I sold all the movable valuables I had. I let things go at cheap prices, just so I could get rid of them and get the house emptied out. What I couldn't sell, I threw away. In the midst of this, I also threw away papers that I sorely needed later.

Finally, some people appeared who were interested in leading the natural life and had formed an association. The association wanted to take the farm—for only a down payment. I had to enter into a contractual agreement that made me part of the association; that's the only way the transaction could work.

I moved into the Buddhist monastery in Sydney where Phra Khantipalo was now living. There was a house there for lay people where I could live. Every two weeks I had to go back to the farm and restore some order to things there. This was completely indispensable. The association was incapable of maintaining the many systems related to the garden and the farm. True, its members wanted to live the natural life, but they did not have much interest in working while they were doing it. Thus many things seriously deteriorated, including the glorious rose garden we had put in.

Phra Khantipalo asked me to help him with teaching. I gave my first course alone on the farm—in the garage that Gerd and I had enlarged and fitted out together. About ten participants showed up, and I taught them how to meditate. I did quite a good job of it, and that gave me pleasure.

Gerd wrote to Jeff. At that point in time, Gerd was in Israel. He did not stay there, though. In the time that followed, he traveled around a great deal. Today he owns four hectares of land in Nepal, where he has planted hundreds of trees.

For about half a year, I fought against my problems and was unhappy. Then I woke up one morning on the farm, and I saw, as if scales had fallen from eyes, how ridiculous it was for me myself to be making myself unhappy. All I had to do was simply say (or think): things are as they are, and however they are is okay.

At that moment I dropped everything that had accumulated in me in the way of bitterness and frustration. I, so to speak, stepped out of my negative feelings. Since that time, I have never again knowingly made myself unhappy. And I was and still am capable of communicating this approach to other people. I can at least explain it to them. Whether or not they can go on to accomplish it too depends on their capacity for arousing will power.

At last I was actually able to sell our farm, Shalom. We—the association and myself—got a bit of money for it, not much. It was not a good deal. Be that as it may, that worry was now gone.

I now moved to Sydney definitively. Phra Khantipalo wanted to establish a forest monastery, and I now had some money from the sale of the farm as well as having inherited something from my mother, who had died the year before. I invested everything I had in the monastery, Wat Buddha Dhamma. Phra Khantipalo and I, after months of searching, found a suitable place in the middle of a national park—seventy hectares, about the size of Shalom.

Phra Khantipalo was the abbot. I worked on organization. And both of us did the teaching. Many buildings

My kuti *(hut) at* Wat Buddha Dhamma.

came into existence, including a splendid meditation hall.
A lovely *kuti* was built for me on a cliff. Little by little,
more and more *kutis* were built for people who came to
this place to live a spiritual life, to enter the path of inner
contemplation.

Enough people came to assure the continued existence of Wat Buddha Dhamma. Everyone participated in
the building costs. This institution has now been in existence for more than twenty years. At first Phra Khantipalo and I were the trustees. Today we have four trustees.
I am represented by one of my students.

From this point onward, the teaching of the Buddha
determined my entire life. In accordance with this teaching, there are four major efforts to be made. Here they
are, expressed as a formula:

- Not permitting unwholesome thoughts to arise that have not yet arisen—in a word, avoiding
- Not engaging further in unwholesome thoughts that have already arisen—in a word, overcoming
- Arousing a wholesome thought that has not yet arisen—in a word, developing
- Engaging further in a wholesome thought that has already arisen—in a word, maintaining

Avoiding, overcoming, developing, maintaining: this is the gateway to the spiritual life.

This means paying attention to oneself and recognizing the content of one's own thoughts. If these thoughts are negative, filled with rejection, hate, irritation, and aversion, one realizes that through them one is harming oneself and making oneself unhappy. Through meditation, one learns to replace such thoughts with their opposites. The opposites are positive, loving, helping thoughts.

Now, it is not always immediately possible to switch thoughts in this manner. It is not so simple. How to do this has to be learned. In making this switch, it is important to take small intermediary steps. You must let go of the negativity and unwholesomeness that have come over you to the point where you are able to think about something beautiful—a beautiful meadow with flowers growing in it or a beautiful piece of music. Or you can think about a person you love. In this way, your thoughts are directed toward something that brings joy to your mind and feelings.

Once this has happened, you can go back again to the original thoughts and try to replace them. You had become irritated about somebody. Now you can also recognize what is good in that person.

It became clear to me that this ability was indispensable for entry into the teaching of the Buddha and for the process of spiritual growth. Even when I did not yet have a precise knowledge of the teaching, I already felt this intuitively. I knew within me that the process of making oneself unhappy is a kind of insanity to which we all fall prey all too easily.

In the Shanghai days after the end of the war, I made an effort in my inmost heart not to think of Germany in a hate-filled way, but to reconcile myself with the Germans and Germany. I sensed that thoughts of hatred could achieve nothing more than casting an unwholesome dark cloud over my life. Much later I found expressed with great clarity in the teaching of the Buddha exactly what I had felt earlier in an unclear way.

These four major efforts are four of the thirty-seven factors of enlightenment. No course or talk I give fails to have these instructions woven into it. They are of the greatest importance. Once you have practiced these instructions long enough, it becomes a habit not to let unwholesome thoughts arise. You avoid them. This does not mean that you suppress them.

Many people today think like this: I should not suppress anything, I must let everything in me come out. At the moment, this is a very fashionable idea. But here it is not a matter of suppressing but of avoiding. We should not let everything in us have its way. We have both good and evil in us. And only if we develop the good will the evil in us one day disappear.

Another major theme in the Buddhist teaching is letting go. The path to letting go is found in the five daily considerations. Every day one should consider the following:

- I am subject to decay, I cannot escape decay.
- I am subject to illness, I cannot escape illness.
- I am subject to death, I cannot escape death.
- Everything that is mine and is dear to me must change and disappear.
- I am the possessor of my karma, the inheritor of my karma; whether I create good or bad karma, I will be the inheritor of that karma.

"Everything that is mine and is dear to me must change" relates particularly aptly to our relationship with our children and partners. Children begin changing from the day they are born. But they disappear or they can disappear. The same is true of partners.

None of us really *believes* that our children or partner belong to us. Nevertheless we *feel* that way about them and want to hold on to them. The various relationship problems in families arise out of this.

We would like to be able to control our partners. We think we have to determine the way our children develop. We think we can decide what they should and should not do. We not only want to keep our children and partners for ourselves, but we think they should live in accordance with our wishes and our conception of them. And none of this is true.

We have to let go if we want to live and love in freedom. Not even one's own body is "mine," the Buddha said, so how can another person be "mine"? Everyone creates his or her own karma.

At this point I would like to explain a small part of the teaching of the Buddha that relates directly to me—and as I know from my work—to very many other people.

Pure love is love that has no wish to hold and to keep but is simply given freely. Over the years I have learned this more and more deeply.

In 1979 I decided to become a nun.

Up until that time, I had tried a lot of things and had seen that the world cannot make one happy. In the course of our travels it became clear to me that tranquillity and peace have nothing to do with the most beautiful places on earth or the most interesting experiences. They are only to be found in one's own heart.

I was now ready to devote myself to the highest ideal.

It is hard to attain a human birth,
Hard is the life of mortal beings;
It is hard to get to hear the good Dhamma,
Hard it is for buddhas to be born.
—Dhammapada, verse 182

Ilse Becomes Ayya Khema

I have to reach back into the history of my life to describe the rather convoluted paths I traveled before I found what I was looking for.

Before I came in contact with Buddhism at all, I sought for a way within my own religion. I was born a Jew, and although I had no Jewish upbringing in the Orthodox sense, I nevertheless had a connection with things Jewish and to Jewish belief.

When you are born Jewish, you also feel Jewish. This is something that is not necessarily derived from a sense of religious affiliation. In my opinion this feeling has an ethnic basis. When I am anywhere among people I do not know and I get into a conversation with someone, I instinctively know if that person is Jewish like me or not. There's "something in the air" by which we know each other.

When Jeff was thirteen years old, we took him to see a rabbi. At this age, boys celebrate their bar mitzvah, their entry into adulthood. Gerd, who had been brought up Orthodox, introduced himself by his Hebrew name. I had no idea whether I had a Hebrew name or not. The rabbi gave me a long look and said, "Are you Jewish at all?"

Gerd said, "Yes, of course she's Jewish. It's just that she isn't educated about it." Then we quickly thought up a name for me. I had no knowledge at all in this area.

For a period of time I did my best to make up for this and gain the knowledge I lacked. I read lots of books, for example, the *Zohar* and other books about the Kabbalah. But I understood little of this. It was on a level to which I had no access. Then, while we were still living on Shalom, I heard of an international organization called Chabad that taught mystical Hasidic Judaism. The seat of this organization in Australia was in Sydney. I looked up the teacher there. He was a mathematics professor at the University of Sydney. He had a wife and six children and gave teachings every evening in his home.

I listened to him and understood that in order to enter into this mystical teaching, to begin with one had to have a more or less perfect command of Hebrew. I knew just the most important prayers by heart, but I couldn't speak Hebrew at all, let alone read it. In addition to that, I would have had to adopt an Orthodox life style. That would have meant keeping a kosher household, which was an impossibility for me, since I didn't even know the basic principles. And the third thing was that I would have had to be a man. That was in any case beyond my reach. To put the matter more precisely, as a woman I would have been allowed to listen, but not participate.

I also wrote to Gershom Scholem, a modern interpreter of the Kabbalah whose books I had read. He had been a professor at the Hebrew University in Jerusalem, but had now retired and was living in Switzerland. I asked him for help in making a connection to the Kabbalah and the *Zohar*. He wrote back immediately and told me that until about thirty years previous there had been a school that taught this path outside of Jerusalem. The name of it had been Beth El (House of God), but it had closed down for lack of next-generation teachers and sufficient interest. That is when I gave up on this path.

Not long ago, an interesting book fell into my hands, called *The Jew in the Lotus*. It tells of a conference in Dharamsala, the Dalai Lama's seat in exile. The Dalai Lama had invited a Jewish delegation of rabbis and leaders of Jewish organizations to visit him. They were supposed to explain to him how the Jewish people had managed to preserve its identity and religion through two thousand years of exile. After all, this is a burning question today for the Tibetans.

What particularly touched me was the description of the meeting that took place between these conference participants and dozens of people of Jewish extraction who had been ordained as monks and nuns in the Tibetan tradition. These monks and nuns were now living and studying in Dharamsala. All of them had the same story to tell as I did. They had searched for the deeper, mystical aspect of their own religion, and then, when they found no way of making a connection with it, they had turned, full of faith, to Buddhism.

The decision to become a Buddhist nun was not an easy one for me. Before I reached it definitively, I did a three-month rainy-season retreat in a monastery in Thailand. In the months of August, September, and October, it rains continuously in India, and in Thailand it rains a great deal. The rainy-season retreat always starts on a full-moon day; thus the date in our calendar shifts a little year by year.

The Buddha set aside this season as a time for monks and nuns to remain in their monasteries and occupy themselves with meditation and study. Food was to be brought to the monasteries for them. The reason for this, as so often with the Buddha, was a very pragmatic and enlightened one. He was always surrounded by a large number of monks and nuns, who every day set out across the countryside, over the fields, with their alms bowls in hand in order to go from house to house begging for food. In the rainy season, the farmers came to the Buddha and complained that these hosts of monks and nuns spreading out across the countryside trampled the newly planted rice sprouts, which were not visible because they were planted under water. In a very real way the lives of the farmers depended on the well-being of these plants.

The Buddha decided that this could not continue. The simplest countermeasure was to keep the monks and nuns in their monasteries. From this arose this custom of the rainy-season retreat, which continues to this day. Here in the West we have changed the time of year of this retreat to correspond with our own weather. We keep the retreat in the wintertime, when the snow and ice are on the ground and it is also a good time to stay inside.

So I went to Thailand for three months, to a forest

monastery, which was set beautifully among the trees. There a famous monk by the name of Tan Ajahn Singtong taught, whose eighty-year-old mother lived with a few nuns in the part of the monastery set aside for women. He visited her every day and gave a Dharma talk, which was translated for me.

I tried to learn Thai, but because I am not at all musical, this was hopeless. Thai is a tonal language. The same word can have five different intonations and five different meanings. I was simply unable to distinguish them. For many people apparently, this is quite easy.

I remember three experiences from this time of retreat. First was sitting on the wooden floor for meditation without a cushion and with legs crossed. This is something that has to be learned, and it took me quite a while to do so.

Something else, which had a strange effect on me, was seeing the Buddhist inhabitants of the surrounding country expressing their veneration for the Buddha and the monks by carrying large quantities of food to the monastery daily. This is a custom that I did not adopt later in the monasteries I founded myself. It was not for nothing that the Buddha declared that he did not want a religion of food. Thus I also did not adopt various other traditions.

Then I also had to stand by and see what a subordinate position the nuns in Thailand occupy. They weren't even called nuns but rather "ladies in white." I was not excited about this.

I spent the second part of my rainy-season retreat in another forest monastery where Tan Ajahn Mahabova lived, an enlightened man, I was told.

Both Tan Ajahn Singtong and Tan Ajahn Mahabova were wonderful teachers. I have much to be grateful to them for. There is a story that is told about the two of them. When King Bhumipol of Thailand was celebrating his sixtieth birthday, he invited the most famous monks of his country to the celebration, including these two. Tan Ajahn Mahabova sent a message to the king saying, "If he wants to see me, he should come here." Tan Ajahn Singtong accepted the invitation and with nine other monks, boarded the airplane the king sent for them. The plane crashed, and they were all killed. That happened ten years after I had been there.

My time in the two forest monasteries was a very profound experience for me. In both places, I had the great good fortune of getting good translations of the Dharma talks. But the difficulty of the language and the subordinate position of the nuns were enough to discourage me from being ordained as a nun there. How often I had seen the nuns spending their entire morning cooking for the monks! I had already cooked every day for my family for more than thirty years, so this did not strike me as an attractive prospect for the future.

Back in Australia, I said to Phra Khantipalo, "I want to be ordained a nun, but not in Thailand." I already knew where—in Sri Lanka. I remembered how beautiful it had been there when we drove through—like paradise! And since Sri Lanka had been under British rule for over a hundred years, many people there spoke English.

At this point, I would like to come back to the subject of what moved me to become a nun. I was fifty-five years old and had seen the world. I had children and I had grandchildren. I had been married. I had money. I

The last photograph of me before I became a nun.

had been poor and for a while also rich. I had had a farm and Shetland ponies. I had experienced the life of suburban America and also lived in a trailer with a camp stove and a fold-up bed. I had been a secretary in a bank and my son's private teacher. Thus I had more or less had and tried everything. What did the world still have to offer me? The world does not bring one inner peace and inner happiness, because everything that happens in the world is impermanent.

All the things I have just enumerated are past and gone. Everything I have recorded in this book is memory, and there is much that I cannot even remember anymore. It has simply vanished from the stream of time.

I had lived what could be called an eventful life. I

hadn't planned it that way, it had just come about on its own. Where should I still seek anything other than within myself? The moment had come to say goodbye to the world. That sounds like it means withdrawing completely from things, which of course I have done from time to time. But we cannot withdraw entirely from the world. As long as we have a body, we have to live in the world. We have to feed this body, we have to talk, we have to have contact with other people.

And on top of that: when you teach, the students who come to you bring the world with them.

By "saying goodbye to the world," I only mean entering into a new phase of experience in which you experience the world as an observer, not as one who continues to be drawn into its passions. This is not something you can always accomplish at the beginning, but in the end it works better and better. The observer has a lot of sympathy and love for the people around him, but he no longer permits himself to become entangled in their feelings and destinies.

There is a very beautiful word: compassion. That means that at the beginning one has empathy for those who have passions. But the goal of the Buddhist teaching is to get rid of these passions. For the passions draw us into hatred and greed.

Teachers try to communicate this to their students, and in teaching they themselves learn it ever more deeply. Only if in teaching you experience yourself as still learning do you have what people call authority. Only if that is the case do you touch people's hearts. They have to feel that this person who talks so cleverly has also been through learning himself, has accomplished something that I can emulate; this person does not talk like a book, but from the heart.

Becoming a nun was for me the next logical step in my development. Today I see that my past had led me onto this path. My experiences made it possible for me to let go of a great deal of personal fear, fear for my own life and fear for that of my fellow human beings. I have seen that it is possible to deal with any situation in life, whether it is in the Amazon basin or in the thin air of Hunza. You can get through anything if you just go with the flow of events.

I have learned to discipline myself in matters of bodily comfort. For me, that was an enormous advance. In my childhood I was spoiled by the ultimate in comfort. In Shanghai, my parents provided me with a home just like in the old days. In America as a young woman, I lived in as much comfort as a lovely suburban house could provide.

And then the comfortable life came to an end. I learned to sleep on the beach with the mosquitoes, to travel a river in incandescent heat in a hollowed-out tree trunk. On the crossing from Java to Sumatra, we were aboard a steamer that was in reality a cattle-transport ship and on which there no places to sit or to lie down. There I stretched out on the wooden planks and slept soundly.

I never mourned for the loss of my comfort, because I learned you can also do without. That was a really important learning process, a letting go of outer conditions. And that brought a great deal of inner freedom; it lifted me up to a level where the spiritual aspect of life had priority.

So I flew to Sri Lanka. Phra Khantipalo gave me a letter to the Ven. Nyanaponika Thera, one of the most famous monks in Sri Lanka, who lived in a small hut outside of Kandy. Nyanaponika Thera was a German Jew who had been a monk since 1935. Because of our common background, we immediately had a good rapport with one another. He was an especially lovable and loving person, a meditator and a great scholar, who had made many translations from the Pali texts of the original words of the Buddha.

Pali only exists in the Buddha's discourses, the rules of the order, and in the Abhidhamma. Thus it is a dead language and does not even have its own alphabet.

The Buddha's words were written down for the first time approximately two hundred and fifty years after his death, using the Singhalese alphabet and on palm leaves. There is a monastery in Sri Lanka that continuously copies these palm leaves and creates new ones, because they keep decaying. There always has to be at least one complete edition of all the scriptures of the Pali canon on palm leaves.

Here in the Buddha-Haus im Allgäu we have the Pali canon in English and German translation in our library. My own knowledge of Pali is spotty.

Nyanaponika Thera told me he could ordain me at any time in his little hut, but that this would not be such a formal and beautiful way of doing it as if he were to write his friend the Ven. Narada Thera, who was the head teacher at the big temple in Colombo, a letter of introduction and ask him to do it.

With this letter of introduction, I went to Colombo, which meant a long bus ride that seemed to me no less

Ven. Nyanaponika Thera in front of his small house in Kandy, Sri Lanka. I often visited him to ask questions. He was my first contact in Sri Lanka.

dangerous than the bus rides I'd taken in South America. I introduced myself to Narada Thera. He set a date for my ordination: one day in July of 1979. Then he told me what I had to learn in Pali and pressed the book containing the text into my hand. I already knew most of it. What I still had to learn by heart was not much.

In addition he gave me the address of a place where I could have a nun's habit made. You couldn't buy one ready made.

The nun's habit was made for me by a female tailor from yellow wool. It consisted of a sarong, a skirt that was held in place by a belt, and a little jacket. Over that you wore a further upper cloth, like the one of brown wool I now wear, adapted to the German climate. The fabric for that first habit was the thinnest wool that could be found. The heat in Sri Lanka is often intolerable.

Ven. Narada Thera asked me if I preferred as a nun to bear the name Dhammadinna or the name Khema. I decided quickly. Khema only had two syllables; that would be easier for people from the West to get their minds around.

Later, after I had read and studied a great deal, I found out that in the time of the Buddha, Khema had been a nun whom he called "the nun with the greatest wisdom." She was originally the wife of a king, a very beautiful woman who was also very proud of her beauty. She was not really interested in the Buddha's teaching, in which there were repeated references to the valuelessness of physical beauty. Nevertheless, she went to hear him once more. The Buddha caused her to see a vision of a woman who was more beautiful than she was. And in this vision he caused the woman's face to grow old and lose its beauty, until finally the woman fell over dead. At that moment it became quite clear to Queen Khema that beauty alone meant nothing. The next day she became a nun and later on she also became enlightened. So that is one of the famous stories from the life of the Buddha. I was completely unaware of it when I chose the name.

The monks have a title in front of their names like Phra, Tan, or Ajahn. In front of mine is "Ayya." *Ayya* is the Pali word by which nuns were designated at the time of the Buddha. It means "venerable lady." All the Western Theravadin nuns who have been ordained since I was have been called Ayya.

So I became Ayya Khema.

Before I went to the temple to be ordained, my hair was cut by older nuns. At this time I had long, very full, black hair. The ceremony calls for one to hold in one's hand the first tuft of hair that falls when one's head is being shaved. One is supposed to look at the hair in one's hand and think that just seconds ago this hair was "mine." And now it is no more than something to be thrown in the waste basket. I still remember clearly that I felt nothing about this. No regret, nothing.

That was the beginning. In my yellow robe I walked across the courtyard of the temple to the temple itself. I thought I wasn't seeing right: The whole courtyard and the whole hall were full of people. There were between six and seven hundred people. I asked Narada Thera what they were all doing there, and he said, "I invited them all." He invited everyone he knew, everyone who wanted to come, everyone who spoke English. I got so frightened I forgot all my Pali. I couldn't remember a single word of what I was supposed to say.

Narada Thera said every word first for me, and I repeated every word after him. The ordination goes fairly fast. It doesn't last even ten minutes. Then one has to bow to the Buddha, the teacher, and then all the monks present. After that was done, a group of about twenty little girls clad in white approached me. Each one brought me a gift: toothpaste, toothbrushes, handkerchiefs, washcloths, a little book of proverbs. All this completely overwhelmed me. The girls congratulated me. All the guests congratulated me. That lasted for hours. I said thank you countless times.

By the way, nuns and monks in our tradition actually don't say thank you. But I could never get rid of the habit. I was raised that way, and I continued to say thank you. The reason nuns and monks are not supposed to thank lay people who give them something is that it creates especially good karma for the lay people when they are able to make a gift to a monk or nun. Thus the one who gives the gift says thank you, not the recipient.

I continue to say thank you for everything that I receive. Naturally, as a foreigner I had a little more leeway. I did not have to observe strictly every detail and do everything as it had been done from ancient times.

At the end of the congratulations, I stood up, and at that moment a Western monk approached me. His name was Sumedha, and he had been a famous painter in Switzerland before he became a monk and went to Sri Lanka. He said, "Until now you've been having an affair; now you're married." I realized that he was referring to my connection with the Buddha's teaching. I found this was a very good way to describe my nunhood. Now being a nun was my sole task in life. In this moment it became clear to me that I wanted to relate to my existence as a nun in a professional way. That meant not only reading the teaching of the Buddha but also learning part of it by heart and putting it into practice step by step.

From this a teaching activity arose that has led me to every part of the globe. Today there are thousands of students to whom my personal experiences are communicated through courses, books, and cassettes as practical help for their lives.

Celibacy, being entirely free for this task, is the most important rule of monastic life. For novice nuns, which is what I was, there are altogether ten rules of virtue. They are comprised of the same five rules that I originally heard from Phra Khantipalo—with the difference that the third is changed to the rule of celibacy—plus the following:

- Not eating at the wrong time
- Not dancing, singing, or attending performances
- Not wearing perfume or jewelry; not using cosmetics
- Not sleeping in luxurious beds
- Not engaging in any business for the purpose of personal profit

There have only been novice nuns in Sri Lanka since the beginning of this century. To explain this, I have to go back in history a bit. Traditionally, a nun is only considered fully ordained when she has been received into the order by fully ordained monks and nuns. She then acquires the status of a *bhikkhuni*. Now, the order of *bhikkhunis* died out in Sri Lanka thousands of years ago. Thousands of nuns are mentioned in the ancient chronicles. They lived in huge convents. Then, suddenly, all of that was over. At that time there was already war between the Tamils and the Singhalese, and perhaps the nuns were the most vulnerable and were killed or starved to death. In any case, they disappeared.

Thus there were no more fully ordained nuns, and so I couldn't become a *bhikkhuni* in Sri Lanka, but only a novice nun. I received the full ordination only later, in California. There are nuns in the Zen tradition, in the Tibetan tradition, and in the Theravada tradition. I'm a Theravada nun. I feel most at home in this tradition.

Theravada Buddhism is the fundamental Buddhism, the original Buddhism. Thailand and Sri Lanka, Burma and Cambodia are Theravada countries. It was the original quality of this teaching, straight from the Buddha, that fascinated me from the very beginning:

After my ordination I went to a monastic center specializing in meditation half an hour outside of Colombo, a place called Kanduboda. I had a need for peace and quiet. There I moved into a little cell with a bed, a chair, and a nightstand. We had electric light and a common shower. Wake-up was at four in the morning. With the heat of Sri Lanka, it's very easy to get up at four in the morning. It is a lovely cool time of day, and the sky is already getting light.

I remember my first morning. During meditation, an image came into my mind. A nun was standing there—she looked like a Singhalese—and I knew it was me. I was standing behind a stupa waiting. Quite obviously I had a rendezvous, in fact with a monk, who also appeared. It was a big stupa in the jungle. I saw all the details with great precision.

It was the kind of situation from which I could draw the conclusion that I had ceased to be a nun. And now I was intending to continue something I had begun in a previous life.

The vision was very powerful. One day I told the abbot of this monastery about it. I described the stupa. He said: "You could go and see that one; it's in the forest in the vicinity of Anuradhapura. From your description you could find it easily." In fact I did find it. It looked exactly as I had seen it during meditation, in every detail.

I liked my cell. I could meditate very well there. One day a woman visited me. She invited me to attend a conference of Singhalese nuns and help them to organize themselves. I was perfectly willing to go, but I had only been a nun for a few days, so what business did I have taking on a role there? My visitor told me that the nuns lacked the ability to organize. It was urgently necessary to create an institution that would give the order of nuns more weight. This would help them in their demand for better education and suitable lodgings. Up to this point, nuns had been given the most minimal consideration, treated almost as though they had no worth at all.

I did take part in this conference. Only one of the women present could speak English. With her help I put forward my suggestions. I do not know if anything ever came of them. But I saw that it was an important mission to stand by the nuns there and support them with what we Westerners call know-how.

In another case I succeeded in this. Through a very helpful woman, who today is a friend of mine, I came to know of a monastery in Madiwela, a suburb of Colombo. "Monastery" is already a somewhat grandiose term for the place. The nuns had only a tiny house, which didn't even have a kitchen.

There I made donations that helped to build a large hall in which the nuns could meditate and that had room for a library and two sleeping rooms. I moved into one of the sleeping rooms. We built a kitchen—that is, the work was done by Singhalese construction workers who could not speak a word of English. It was an incredibly nerve-wracking job to direct them in their work.

We took care of getting teachers to visit the hall, which could also be used as a place for study. A plaque was put up on the building with my name on it, and there was a marvelous day of consecration with much singing and chanting from the little schoolgirls and with many nuns present. I established a day of meditation every second Sunday for the English-speaking people in the area. They came in large numbers; the program was always full. I explained how to meditate and why it is done. People brought their lunches, and the nuns made and served tea. Through this, I made friends with many Singhalese women, and some of these friendships still go on today. Some of the women write me once a year, some more often.

At the time of my ordination, I was already a grandmother. My first grandchild, Matthew, my daughter's son, was born in 1973. At the time of my ordination, Jeffrey had finished with university and was already living with Susan, whom he later married. During my initial period as a nun, he got his first job in England, as a computer specialist for the University of Norfolk.

When I left Sri Lanka to return to Australia, I visited him in Norfolk. Once you are already in a plane, the distances you fly don't seem to matter so much.

On the way back, I stopped in India, because I wanted to go to Bombay to see Sri Nisargadatta Maharaj, the sage with the little cigarette shop. I had heard that his teachings were very helpful. Even though I had his address, he was not easy to find.

Finally I got to a street where every person on the street immediately, without being asked, pointed to a little decrepit house, which had a little shop on the street level that was open and had cigarettes and sweets for sale. Without a word a woman indicated with a hand gesture the stairway to the first floor. In a little room, filled to the bursting point with Western visitors, sat Nisargadatta Maharaj on a small platform with two translators at his side. I had barely managed to make sitting room for myself on the floor when Sri Nisargatta began to ask me questions.

With Phra Khantipalo at Wat Buddha Dhamma in Australia.

This was embarrassing for me. I had come to hear his words of wisdom and did not want to talk about myself in front of all those people. But he gave me no peace. He asked me my name and where I came from, about my teachers and my spiritual practice, and at the end he said I was on the right path but not enlightened yet.

Later I found out that he always behaved this way with newcomers. I kept visiting him for a week and found his presentations hard to follow. In retrospect, I would like to say that he was so sure of what he was about and so fervently engaged in it that it was hard to see him as an enlightened person. Three years after my visit he died. He was already over eighty.

Back in the forest monastery in Australia, I helped Phra Khantipalo in the usual way with teaching and organization. One occasion at Wat Buddha Dhamma was of particular significance for me. It was a full-moon evening and we were getting ready as usual to meditate through the night. As I sat in the meditation hall, I was getting more and more tired and more and more bored. We had already sat there for four hours, had chanted, had heard a talk from Phra Khantipalo, and now it was midnight. Then I recalled what I had read about meditative absorptions in the Buddha's discourses. I already had practiced the first, fine-material absorptions that bring delight, joy, and calm, and they were quite familiar to me. But I had not yet experienced the formless absorptions, and there was also no one anywhere who could explain or teach them.

Then it occurred to me that I should just once try to realize infinite space, infinite consciousness, the realm of nothingness, and neither perception nor nonperception. And lo and behold, the level of concentration I already had at my disposal was sufficient to allow me to experience these levels of consciousness. Now my great fatigue and boredom were over, and I remained happily sitting in the meditation hall until six o'clock in the morning.

I meditated in this way until, in 1983, I met Ven. Naññarama Thera, who confirmed for me that I had been practicing correctly and requested me to teach this kind of meditation in the West.

I was drawn to return to Sri Lanka. I saw a big field for meaningful work there. I wanted to help the native nuns get onto their feet, so to speak, to support them, provide them with ideas for how they could get out of the shadows in which they lived. The women I had met in Madiwela wanted to help me with this.

One day I was invited to Polgasduwa. This is an island in Lake Ratgama in the south of the country on which monks live. Ven. Nyanatiloka Thera, the first German Buddhist monk, founded this island monastery in 1911. He was the abbot there. Ven Nyanaponika Thera was his student. Also another famous monk, Lama Govinda—he was also German—lived there for a time. Almost all Western monks in Sri Lanka find their place there.

During my visit the abbot expressed his interest in organizing a meditation course for his monks. He didn't want to give the course himself; he felt I should do it. However, before this came about, it was pointed out that monks were forbidden to listen to the teachings of a nun. A nun was not permitted to teach monks. Thus only lay people could take part in my course. But my talks were recorded on tape, and the monks were then allowed to listen to the cassettes.

The lay people I taught were *dayakas*. That is the Singhalese word for donors and patrons who see to the needs of a monastery and its inmates by providing money, food, and medical help. Part of this group was a Mr. Arthur de Silva, who together with his wife owned an inn on the lakeshore directly across from the island. They were a very, very sweet and kind couple. Today neither one of them is alive.

One day Arthur mentioned an idea to me that I had just had myself shortly before. I had noted that not far from the monk's island, in the same lake, was another island. It had occurred to me that if monks could live here, nuns could live there. Then Arthur asked me what I thought of building a convent for nuns on the second island. I asked him, "Are you thinking that I should then live in that convent?" He said, "Of course. I'll take on designing the buildings, hiring and supervising the workers, and I'll get the materials. I'll also try to get donations."

That is the way our collaboration began, which continued fruitfully until his death in 1989 and brought happiness to us both.

A person, one who has done good deeds,
Also goes on to the next world.
There his good works receive him
As kinsmen welcoming a dear one home.
—Dhammapada, verse 220

The Nuns' Island

I would like to create a kind of memorial here to a man without whom the plan to build a convent on the island never would have been realized: Arthur de Silva from Dodanduwa.

One rarely meets a person like Arthur de Silva. He was a Singhalese with remote Portuguese ancestry. He spoke perfect English and gave all the force he had to the building of the convent. He told me that at the moment of his death he would be contented with his life, because he had been able to help bring the nuns' island into existence.

He bought every nail and every screw and transported everything to the island in a boat he had had made from a giant tree trunk. He hired the workers and made sure through the whole time of construction that they worked in an orderly fashion and didn't waste any material. People familiar with Asia will realize what a difficult task this is.

During most of the time the convent was being built, I was traveling, giving talks and courses in every possible corner of Australia, South Africa, Indonesia, America, and for the first time, in Germany. Whatever donations I received I sent to Arthur de Silva.

I would like recall here the story of a fateful encounter I had during my time on Bali. There is a marvelous Buddhist temple there, kept by a monk who asked me if I wouldn't give a course there for tourists. For in fact, a great number of interested people visited there. I agreed, he posted announcements of the course everywhere, and in fact seven people showed up: five Germans and two Americans.

The temple was magnificent. Its wooden doors were decorated with scenes from the life of the Buddha. There were freshwater springs, fabulous stone figures, tropical flowers all around, and inside was one of the most impressive Buddha statues I'd ever seen.

I taught in English for seven days. On the second day I took a closer look at one of the participants and had the feeling that he hadn't understood a single word. He was German and his name was Charlie, that much I knew.

I asked him if he could understand what I was saying. "No," he admitted. He knew no English. After that, I gave the early morning talk in English and the evening talk in German. I remember that this week I was in very bad health. I had some sort of infection and could neither eat nor drink. But I did not want to disappoint the participants, so I continued with the course. When it comes down to it, their interest gave me pleasure.

Charlie and his friend were particularly attentive and interested students. The others sometimes missed a day, but Charlie and Norbert were always there. After the early departure of the two Americans, I continued the course in German.

My meeting with Charlie and Norbert was a meaningful one for my later life. Norbert was the brother of the monk Nyanabodhi, who has lived with us here in the Buddha-Haus im Allgäu since the beginning. I met him through Norbert under his Western name, Roland. Without those two brothers and without Charlie, our Buddha-Haus wouldn't exist. They were the main ones who requested that I come to Germany from Sri Lanka. They helped with the building work here, and both Norbert and Charlie now teach in our city center in Munich. Nyanabodhi is the abbot of our forest monastery.

But now back to the convent and Arthur de Silva. He kept track of all the money I sent him, down to the last penny. I wasn't that interested in keeping such close track of it—I trusted him completely. But he insisted on it. He was highly conscientious and placed a great deal of emphasis on our figuring out everything precisely. He was an engineer by profession. He was able to draw up all the construction plans himself and of course, unlike me, he could communicate with the construction workers in their mother tongue.

From the moment we became acquainted with one another, we talked as though we had known each other our whole lives. Visitors to the nuns' island even noticed with what implicit understanding we spoke to each other.

The rock in my kuti *becomes a meditation seat.*

We thought this must surely be a connection from a previous life.

Six *kutis* were built on the island—huts for nuns. They were very lovely: Each one had a large room, a bathroom, and a little garden with a wall around it. The entrance was protected by a little projecting roof so that during the rainy season you wouldn't get soaked the moment you stepped out.

In a secluded part of the island I had picked out a favorite spot. My *kuti* was to go there. On the ground there lay a big flat rock. We planned to build my hut around this rock, so that it could be my meditation seat. This all took place according to plan.

Then Arthur de Silva notified me, "You can come now." I flew from Australia, where I was at the time, to Sri Lanka. The first women who moved into the convent with me were my German students.

Everything there was still far from finished. We still had no kitchen and no dining room. We had to cook outdoors on little camp stoves that seemed to have an undue number of technical problems. We also ate outdoors.

Around us the construction work went on. A big building took shape that contained a kitchen, a dining room, a library, a small entry hall, and a storeroom in which the cook could sleep. All around the house, in accordance with the colonial style, was a shady veranda. The house still looks the same today as it did then.

We put flowerpots on the veranda, and the house looked just beautiful. By way of dotting the last *i*, I had a lotus pond put in. I love lotuses. Here in Germany, I have water lilies in their place. Both flowers come from the same family and fairly closely resemble each other. The lotus has a close symbolic connection with the Buddha. Figures of him are often seated on stylized lotuses, for the lotus is the symbol of purity and inviolability. This is in part because the petals of the lotus have the property that water runs off them like so many beads, so they never become wet through. In addition lotuses are used as a simile for spiritual growth, because though they grow out of the slime, their leaves and flowers rise above it, untouched by any impurity.

After the German women, a Singhalese woman came to our convent. During the years I was there, she was my student. She went on to receive ordination on the island. For this occasion, I summoned the monks from the other island. In addition I invited the lay people from the surrounding area to come. More than two thousand people came. I hadn't expected that many. I thought to myself, under that weight, the whole island will sink into the lake. However, fortunately, that did not occur. Naturally, we also had little girls in white dresses with gifts there.

This nun is now my successor as abbess of the convent. She does her job very well. I am glad that both the monastery in Australia that I founded with Phra Khantipalo and the convent in Sri Lanka will continue to exist without me.

That is also what I am striving for in the Buddha-Haus here in the Allgäu—that without me it will remain a place where people come together in the name of the Buddha. After all, I don't know how much longer I will live. Someone said to me, all the same, it would be good if I could stay around a little while longer.

In the beginning we were just a few women on the island, but then it became more and more popular. Since I had been teaching abroad, I had become somewhat well known. The story of my convent in Sri Lanka started to go the rounds.

We built a guesthouse with six rooms, each for two people. In case of need, we could put a third bed in each room. Thus there was room for eighteen people.

In the six *kutis* three nuns and I lived. Two *kutis* were kept available for women who came to us to learn something of the teaching of the Buddha.

Many of the women, including the Germans, stayed for a year and a half. Others came for only a few days. Soon I put a stop to those very short stays by establishing a minimum stay of three months. Otherwise the place would have been like a railway station. That much in-and-out we couldn't deal with. Also, there is no way to work systematically with people visiting that briefly.

In spite of the heat, we had a rigorous schedule. Still in those temperatures accommodations have to be made, otherwise you simply can't endure. We got up at four in the morning, chanted the traditional texts in Pali and English, then we meditated, and then we had breakfast. I always had a cook there who served us, but also each day one of the visitors had to help with the meal.

In the hours before noon we worked. We published a newsletter that had to be sent out. In addition, of course, there was cleanup, the flowers had to be watered and the flowerbeds had to be weeded. The library had to be put in order, covers had to be made for the books, letters had to be written—there was always plenty to do, and in the heat every movement is difficult. Then there was lunch. After that, for an hour I taught the disciplinary rules of the order, the Vinaya.

The women who were with us were so-called *anagarikas*, that is, they were temporary nuns. But even if they were going to leave the monastic life, the rules were of interest for them. I tried to make the Vinaya interesting by interspersing with the rules themselves the stories that explained why the Buddha had made them. For of course, at the beginning, when he first ordained monks and nuns, there were no rules at all. They were all enlightened people, who required no instruction. Only later, when thousands more were added, did there have to be fixed rules.

In the afternoon, each woman could do what she wanted—rest, sit under a tree and meditate, read, or write.

Then in the evening I would give a Dharma talk. From these Dharma talks, three little books were made. The first one was called *Be an Island unto Yourself*. It was in English, because I taught in English there. I had it printed with money from donations and distributed it free of charge. It was my first book, and it is still being reprinted today, here in Germany too. Of course I can't distribute it free of charge anymore, because the printing costs are too high. In the meantime, twenty-five books have been made from my talks. They are in German and English and have been translated into seven languages.

We kept strictly to this daily schedule. When twenty women, and sometimes more, live together, a well-ordered program must be adhered to. Even with such a program, it was not easy to deal with the different personalities and points of view.

Most of the women were from Western countries. Singhalese women who came to us were often not in agreement with the Western way of doing things. After all, the two cultures are entirely different.

Arthur de Silva was a protecting angel and continued to be of the greatest help to me. All the newcomers arrived at his house. He took care of the boat by which they were brought to the island. He listened to complaints and fulfilled whatever wishes lay in his power to fulfill. When Jeffrey and his wife Susan visited me on the island, they lived with Mr. and Mrs. de Silva and were thoroughly spoiled by them.

The abbot of the monastery on the neighboring island looked after us like a father. Every day he came over to our island with his boat to see if there was anything we needed. He brought us bananas and coconuts, other fruits, vegetables, and rice—everything that benefactors had brought to the island of the monks and was in more than sufficient supply there.

*My meditation
seat—a large rock
on the nuns' island,
Parappuduwa.*

Another part of our life was *pindapat*, the alms
round. This custom has been followed by monks and
nuns since the time of the Buddha's life. It is much practiced in the Thai forest monasteries, but had fallen largely
into oblivion in Sri Lanka. This was perhaps because it is
physically a truly taxing affair.

We went by boat to the mainland once a week and
walked—the nuns in front and the *anagarikas* behind—
into the village. In front of every house where someone
signaled us, they had something to put in our alms bowls,
we stopped and held up the bowls to them. Sometimes
we received so much rice that the *anagarikas* had to help
by putting it into one or two buckets, which they carried
for us.

The first time we went, many women came out of
their houses, especially older women, but younger ones
too, to put food into our bowls. They had tears in their

With several nuns doing pindapat *(the alms round) barefoot in Dodanduwa, the biggest village in the neighborhood of the convent.*

eyes and told us how grateful they were to us for providing them with an opportunity to give alms to nuns. Personal contact with a nun meant for them as women the closest connection they could make to the Buddha's teaching. This was my primary reason for reviving the custom. However, we deliberately did not go every day. The population there is very poor; it would have been wrong to make them share their food—and moreover, the best of what they had—with us every day.

Around our lake there were four villages. We visited them by turns, so that each village received a visit from us twelve times a year. That did not seem to me to be too much, especially since they were so happy to see us and to give us alms.

Traditionally, *pindapat* is done barefoot. Sometimes, on the hot black tar of the streets, which burned our feet, or on the hot gravel of the villages, this was not so easy.

I not only wanted us to be accepted by the local people, but I also wanted us to bring some happiness into their difficult lives, which were fraught with hard labor. With this in mind, I paid a visit on the last Sunday of the month to the village from which we had been getting our food all that month. I would come in the company of our Singhalese nun and give a Dharma talk, which she translated. We did this in the time-honored way, as it was done in the time of the Buddha. We sat down under a big tree and waited for our audience to come. The village people came in droves with their children and their whole households. There was always lots of noise and commotion, because there were little children and of course dogs too.

I talked about very simple things—how to behave toward neighbors and spouses, for example, as there was a lot of strife in these villages. The news of it even reached us on our island. The gatherings in the shade of the tree were a good thing, I think. Through them I wanted to express my thanks for the recognition and support I encountered throughout Sri Lanka.

One day, I got word that the prime minister of Sri Lanka wanted to visit us and get meditation instruction from me. Preparing for this visit was a tremendous effort and a great to-do. The road that led through the village to the lakeshore was newly covered with gravel, banners

The premier of Sri Lanka, the Hon. Mr. Premadassa, visits me in my kuti.

were put up everywhere, and the prime minister's body-guard came a day early to subject our island to the most thoroughgoing scrutiny. They looked behind every tree and bush to see if anyone was hiding behind it.

Then the Hon. Mr. Premadasa with his wife and a number of other people arrived on the island, where we were awaiting him at the boathouse. He had us show him my *kuti*, and then we went to the meditation hall to begin with meditation. His intention was to stay for two days.

After I had explained as much as possible to him and we had meditated for twenty minutes, one of his body-guards strode into the hall with heavy steps and indicated that Mr. Premadasa had to return to Colombo as soon as possible, since there was a crisis in the parliament. End of meditation instruction and end of practice.

A few years later, Mr. Premadasa was elected president of Sri Lanka and after a very short time in office was murdered by a terrorist's bomb.

When I was not at the convent, I was abroad giving courses and Dharma talks. For one thing, we needed the money that came in through my teaching to maintain the island. After some time, however, I felt that it would be good for me to pull back from my activities a little. I wanted to do a three-month retreat, just for myself.

Singhalese friends of mine owned a banana plantation in the jungle. On the plantation was an old house, which was in terrible condition but still good enough to provide basic shelter. In this house I spent three months alone. My friends had arranged to have a Tamil servant for me. He couldn't speak a word of English and I couldn't speak a word of Tamil, so a "noble silence" prevailed. I only knew the word for water. I could tell him I needed that. They wanted to provide me with a cook too, but I rejected that idea. It would have only made things more complicated. The servant could go into the village and get me bread, eggs, tomatoes, and cucumbers. That was really completely sufficient. I didn't need hot food every day. I had a large quantity of tea, because my friends had a tea plantation, and besides that there were lots of bananas, coconuts, and pineapple. All these things were on hand.

I made a schedule and meditated a lot. For once I didn't have to worry about the welfare of others, which I experienced as a vacation.

At this time I had already met my most important teacher. This was a very old Singhalese monk of whom I had been told by one of the monks on our nuns' island. No one understood as much about meditation as he did.

In those days in Sri Lanka, it was not usual to cultivate meditation practice. This has changed in the mean-

time, through the influence of English-speaking women, and perhaps I too made some contribution in this
direction.

This old monk, the Ven. Naññarama Thera, was the
abbot of a forest monastery in the middle of the jungle.
After hearing the stories that were circulating about him,
I felt I absolutely had to meet him. The first time I went
to see him, it was at a patron's house in Colombo. He was
staying there because he had been sick. This first visit, in
1983, has remained an unforgettable experience for me.
Of course we had to have a translator and found for this
purpose a nice young monk who was his abbot's atten-
dant and could speak perfect English.

I sat down in front of Ven. Naññarama Thera on the
floor and began to tell him about my meditation experiences. I had already been practicing the meditative absorptions for years, but had never found anyone with
whom I could talk about them and who could confirm to
me that I was on the right track in practicing them. There
and then I found someone who had a complete understanding of the matter.

After a few minutes, during which he listened with
interest, it occurred to me that he did not know me at all
and that therefore I should tell him that I had been already been meditating for twenty years. Otherwise he
might think I had just made these meditation experiences
up or had just had them by accident. After he had had my
remarks about my twenty years of practice translated to
him, he broke into laughter and said something to the
young monk. The young monk turned to me and translated: "Ah so, so she's meditated for twenty years! More
likely twenty lifetimes!"

I continued with my account. By the time I got to the eighth absorption, I didn't really know what I should say about it, so I told him that I would quickly do it rather than risk a false explanation. So I concentrated my mind and went from the first absorption to the eighth one stage by stage, but in just a few minutes.

When I opened my eyes again I saw the Ven. Naññarama Thera looking at me with a combination of astonishment and benevolence. I then described what I had experienced in the eighth absorption. In principle, that should be very little, since on that level the mind rests totally.

Ven. Naññarama Thera confirmed to me that I had correctly practiced and described the absorptions. Then he said that it was my duty to teach these meditative absorptions in the West, and not least for the reason that cultivation of them was a lost art.

I have taken his words to heart and have now been teaching them for many years. To begin with, I hesitated a little to offer this uncommon practice to the public, but as I saw that more and more of my students were attaining the absorptions, I began explaining them more and more precisely. Today they constitute an important part of all my meditation courses.

Later, I often undertook the six-hour trip to his forest monastery to talk with Ven. Naññarama Thera and to receive further strength and guidance from him. I was always warmly welcomed, and he also remembered our first meeting, especially the fast meditation I did in order to give him an account of the eight absorptions.

He wrote a book that was translated from Singhalese into English. It is not a thick book, but in it he describes the entire path of Buddha's teaching—from the beginning up to enlightenment. I took this book with me for my three months on the banana plantation and studied it. Wherever I had a question, I drew a cross. After my retreat, I went to see Ven. Naññarama Thera and went over the book with him word for word. We then translated it into German. That translation was a part of the festschrift for my seventieth birthday.

In the meantime Ven. Naññarama Thera has died. He was ninety-one years old.

The three months of solitude were of the greatest significance for me. I came away from them very much strengthened—ready to share my insights with people who were interested in hearing them. Still today, I have the sounds of the jungle in my ears: the cries of the monkeys and birds and the wind rushing through the banana leaves. But there were also times of utter quiet, at dawn and twilight. I took walks in the jungle in order to look at nature as a part of myself. After all, in the end we are nothing different from nature.

For example, I teach a contemplation of the four elements: earth, fire, water, and wind, the basic elements that comprise us and also comprise nature. And when one places oneself directly in the middle of nature, without the least disturbance, that is a good opportunity to feel oneself as completely connected with it and to experience that we are nothing different from everything existing around us.

Our island became more beautiful with each passing year. In the beginning it was just jungle, with snakes and rats. We put in paths and gardens. The area was not a very big one. The whole island was about a half a kilometer long and a quarter of a kilometer wide. This was all that was needed, but at the beginning most of the women found it difficult to get used to life in this seclusion.

There was no way to get anywhere without getting into a boat. First we had a rowboat. Then a German couple gave us a larger than usual donation so we could buy an outboard motor. Of course that made things much easier, but we first had to learn how to run and maintain the motor.

It was also not easy to find a housekeeper and a cook, especially one who could speak English. Most of them were not happy on the island, being so alone among the foreign women. Finally I found a woman who enjoyed being with us and who stayed with me until the end. She continued for quite a while to send letters to me here frequently.

In some ways our life on the island was an idyllic one, but in another way it was also very hard. We had to deal with the boiling heat, the mosquitoes, and a discipline to which I always paid strict attention. I know that almost all the women who came there benefited from their stay. One of them, for example, now lives in Stuttgart and is the secretary of the Buddha-Haus Association. Another, a Dutch woman, lives in Wat Buddha Dhamma in Australia and is the manager there. I have also authorized her to teach, which she does superbly and with love.

I am continually meeting women who were with me on the island. Many later organized courses for me in their home towns. Teaching more and more became my life.

I still remember the first course I gave in Austria. I had just come from Sri Lanka. Seven people had signed up. I was asked if I would still give the course. I said, "But of course." The next time I offered a course there, twenty-five people came. In Switzerland I once gave a talk to an audience of twelve. Many hundreds of people come to hear my talks today. But the beginning was not like that.

I taught in Switzerland, England, Holland, and Denmark. I taught in South Africa, where there is a very beautiful Buddhist center. And of course I taught again in Australia and in the United States. Everywhere I took the donations I received and used them for the maintenance of the nuns' island. That worked very well.

An interesting year for me was 1987. The first thing was that I was invited by the delegate to the United Nations from Sri Lanka to give a talk at the United Nations in New York. Almost all the representatives of the smaller countries came, but those of the large countries were absent. The United States and Russia were not represented. At the time, the Iron Curtain had not yet been lifted.

I spoke about peace in the heart as a prerequisite for bringing peace to the world, and there were also a great number of questions afterward. But it seemed that those present believed that religion and politics do not go together. In the Buddha's time, he taught many kings and high ministers. Today this is still quite difficult. At the end, I was awarded a small medal for peace, which pleased me a great deal.

The second event of that year was the International Conference for Buddhist Nuns in Bodh Gaya, in India. The Dalai Lama presided over the conference. This was the first time that anything of this nature had taken place, and I was one of the three women who organized the event. The other two were an American nun from the

The first conference for Buddhist nuns took place in 1987 in Bodh Gaya, India. The Dalai Lama presided over the conference. Here he is discussing the situation of nuns with me.

Tibetan tradition and a Thai professor. We founded Sakyadhita (Daughters of the Buddha), an international organization for Buddhist nuns and women. Since then the organization has held a conference nearly every year and has brought about improvements for nuns and relieved some of the difficulties they face, particularly those from Asia.

Above all this organization provides an opportunity for exchange among Buddhist women from more than thirty countries. We learn from each other and about each other. Another very important function is providing support for women who want to become fully ordained *bhikkhunis*.

The year 1988 was marked by an extraordinary event. I flew to California to participate in a *bhikkhuni* ordination ceremony at Hsi Lai Temple in Los Angeles. This was the first time that a ceremony of this nature was possible in the West, and it was even done in the traditional manner with a double platform. This means that we nuns received ordination from both nuns and monks. Two hundred and fifty Chinese nuns, fifty monks, and twelve Western nuns came to the ordination. The Hsi Lai Temple is built in the style of the "Forbidden Palace" in Peking, and many of the assemblies took place in the inner court of the temple. The temple itself had just been finished at a cost of twenty-five million U.S. dollars, as one could learn from a plaque on one of its walls.

We received a rigorous, almost military-style training, almost all in Chinese. We were treated most generously and did not have to pay anything for lodging, food, and clothing. It would have been better if they had immediately established some Western nuns there, since only one of the Chinese nuns spoke English and the temple was intended for the spreading of the Teaching in the West.

After we had received training daily for four weeks, many hours a day, the great day of the ordination arrived. This meant both the day and the night for the nuns, because we had to be ordained twice—once by ten monks, who had all been monks for at least thirty years; and again by ten *bhikkhunis*, who had all been *bhikkhunis* for at least twenty years. We all completed the process successfully, although the Western monks and nuns often had no idea what was going on, because the proceedings were not translated. But we understood the essential. I was glad when it was over, since every bone in my body ached.

One curious thing has remained in my memory. In China and of course in Taiwan also, nuns and monks are

The vows are taken (second from right).

required to be vegetarians. But every day in the temple fabulous food was provided. Once it seemed to be chicken, another time, fish, another time liver. Until one day I got my courage up and asked the English-speaking nun why vegetarian food was not being provided. She looked at me in amazement and told me that of course all the food was vegetarian. When I told her about the chicken and fish, she was highly amused. She explained to me that everything had been made from soy flour and flown in from Taiwan daily, since such things were not available in the West.

Before I flew back to the nuns' island, I stayed for a while with Irene, whom I had not seen for a rather long time. It was lovely for the two of us to be together again. I also have a particular memory from this visit.

Irene asked me why I was a nun. She could under-stand being a Buddhist, but why a nun? Then I asked her if it made her feel good when she went to church with her

Amy arrives at the airport in Los Angeles. Irene has her little girl.

husband, Ronny, on Sundays. She said yes. Then I told her that I wanted to feel that way every day. This answer seemed to satisfy her completely.

By that time I had already had my second grand-child, with whom another story is connected. Irene wanted to have a little girl, but at the same time she also wanted to offer a home and family to a child that had no parents. Thus she and Ronny put in a request for a Ko-rean orphan, but as time went on they received no an-swer. Just at a time when I was visiting her, a letter finally arrived saying that a little girl had been found for her in Korea, and there was a photograph attached. From look-ing at the photo I could plainly see that this was a men-tally handicapped child, and it was clear to me also that this would represent a burden for Irene that she was not truly capable of taking on. In any case I was planning to fly to Korea to visit an Australian nun who was a friend of mine, so I offered to go and meet the little girl. I was able to do this with the help of my nun friend, who fortunately also spoke Korean. We told the bureau of adoption that my daughter didn't wish to take this little girl and that they should look for another one. This was a rather complicated discussion, but it bore fruit, and two months later Amy Jung Ah arrived at the Los Angeles airport with a woman accompanying her. Amy couldn't speak a word of English. She was five years old and had been raised from birth in a Korean orphanage. She not only looked sweet, but she was also extremely well behaved—doubtless she had been well trained in this respect—and she learned English very quickly. Today she is seventeen years old, has stunning looks, is entering her last year of high school, where she is an outstanding student, swims like a fish, has a host of friends, and is coming this year for the first time to visit her grandma. She just wrote me a letter in which she asked me to organize a trip to a concentration camp, since that is something she is now studying in school. Besides that, she want to see King Ludwig's castles.

Unfortunately, terrible unrest began to break out in Sri Lanka. Bomb attacks and terrorist raids made life in this country ever more difficult. For example, buses were regularly blown up. You could no longer travel by bus. A considerable number of post offices were destroyed. You could no longer rely on letters and other mail being forwarded or arriving at all. I, unfortunately, was dependent on the mail system.

The worst thing was that I no longer had the confidence to reply positively to women who wrote from abroad asking to come to the nuns' island. I would have held myself responsible if something had happened to them. The uncertainty was far too great to permit such risks. So I told them not to come. In this way, a part of my work was blocked. A second blockage was the fact that in addition the Singhalese women who were my students no longer dared to leave their houses. The way to us on the island was too dangerous for them.

Then a horrible thing happened. The man who owned the banana plantation where I had done my retreat, a person who was thus my friend and benefactor, was attacked by terrorists and burned alive.

On top of this, there was the death of Arthur de Silva. In 1988, as I was leaving on a trip to California, I had a very strong feeling that I would never see Arthur de Silva again. When I came back, he had in fact died. He was a diabetic and had never been too precise about his diet. One day he fell over dead.

When, in 1989, at the request of my German students, I decided to leave Sri Lanka, surely his death was another factor that reinforced my feeling: my time here is over.

And even if one lives a hundred years
Without composure, without insight,
One day lived by a wise one, a meditator,
Is far better.
—Dhammapada, verse 111

Buddha in the Allgäu

In the spring of 1989, I arrived from Sri Lanka at the Munich airport. Charlie, my non-English-speaking student from Bali, picked me up, and we drove to Uttenbühl. It was raining and cold.

Uttenbühl is a little village with five houses, situated in the middle of very green meadows. At that season, everywhere streams of water from the thawing snows were flowing down from the wooded mountains and over the roads and smaller lanes.

The next-to-last house from the woods, which had an old pear tree in the garden, was my new residence. I found it very beautiful. Donations had made the purchase possible, and the renovation of the house had been in progress since February. The work was mainly being done by my students, who were willing to work without being paid.

The first community group at Buddha-Haus. From the right: Roland, Charlie, Gudrun, and me.

Charlie, a professional tennis coach from Munich; Roland, an interior designer, cabinetmaker, and landscape gardener from Rosenheim; Gudrun, a dance and gymnastics teacher from northern Germany; Heinz, a businessman from Munich; and Norbert, Roland's brother, who had been my student with Charlie that time in Bali—these were the workers, the original team.

I remember the day of my arrival clearly. Everything was lying about—crates of books, suitcases, boxes—and we worked until four in the morning putting things in order. The young people seemed to be astounded by my energy.

We completed the renovation, with the help of professionals, in an incredibly short time. I had arrived in April. In May I gave my first course. If I remember correctly, there were twenty participants. Shortly before the first students arrived, we were still hanging pictures in the rooms and corridors. Then, with relief, we dropped our tools.

For the people from the surrounding area, I arranged an open house for every Wednesday evening. This has remained an established fixture up till the present. I give a Dharma talk, and after that, we meditate. The first Wednesday, five people showed up. Nowadays, between sixty and ninety people regularly come to our Wednesday evenings—just the number of people who can fit into the meditation hall and the adjoining anteroom. Afterward, we have tea with our guests. This is always a very enjoyable time—people open their hearts and talk about the things that are on their minds.

For some years, owing to lack of space, I have held my courses and seminars not at Buddha-Haus, but in Catholic monasteries instead. Here we only have sleeping accommodations for about thirty guests, which has led to long waiting lists, since we often had more than two hundred people signing up.

We are welcome guests at the monasteries. We pay for food and lodging, and "noble silence" prevails at our courses. Beyond that, there is also interest in our work among the monks there. At St. Albert Monastery in Walberberg bei Köln, the prior came to every one of my talks. In Niederaltaich in the Bavarian woods, the abbot himself meditated. He had learned meditation in Japan in a Zen monastery and has written very beautiful books about meditative absorption during prayer. He was beaming as he told us that a number of his monks had watched our walking meditation and then said that they

Abbot Emmanuel from Niederaltaich Monastery, who warmly welcomes my students and me every year for a meditation course.

wanted to try it too. The cloisters that are still to be found in the old monasteries were at one time used for a similar practice.

It is a major concern of mine to develop this ecumenical dialogue and keep it alive. It is not my idea to proclaim Buddhism as the only salvation. I want to show people in Germany that the spiritual path can be traveled within every religion and to help them make a connection to a deeper inner contemplation. I feel the duty to reveal the path that my teachers have shown me to Western people. In this I am helped by the fact that German as well as English are mother tongues of mine, which I have spoken since childhood. This makes it possible for me to express myself with simplicity and directness.

A great deal of the force that I expended during the years of development in Sri Lanka and in Germany arose from the feeling that I had no time to lose. Since 1983 I have known that I have cancer. I felt a lump in my breast and went to see a doctor in Australia. She sent me for a mammogram. Diagnosis: a malignant tumor.

At that time we had just begun with the building of the convent on the island in Lake Ratgama. I really wanted to finish that work and was then feeling completely healthy and strong. I told the doctor that I did not want an operation, because I didn't want to be drawn into the cycle of hospital treatment, which, once one is in it, is hard to get out of. I can still clearly remember that the doctor looked at me for a long time and then told me that her mother had also been ill with breast cancer and had made exactly the same decision. She did not permit herself to be operated on, and she lived fifteen years with the disease. She was only sick for the last two months, and then she died. That suits me fine, I told her. I'd like to do it the same way.

What the illness did for me during the next years was to create the consciousness of urgency—*samvega* in Pali—which the Buddha always recommended. It is the urgency of practicing the spiritual path, because after all nobody knows how long he is still going to live. When you have cancer, you can recognize this even more clearly.

Every birth is a death sentence. There is no one who survives life. We push this sentence out of our minds and live as though we had an infinitely long time before us.

This feeling of urgency motivated me strongly to bring the project of the nuns' island to completion, so that the maximum number of women would be able to practice there under optimal conditions. I also wanted to complete a great number of books in order to make the teaching of the Buddha available in German to as many people as possible. When I was young, I made up my mind that sometime I would write a great novel. I had a glorious vision of holding in my hand a book I had written myself. I never did get around to writing a novel, but by now twenty-five books of mine have been published, and it is no longer anything special for me to sign my own book. But I am happy that, through these books, the Dharma is being spread. The Buddha did not call his doctrine Buddhism but Dharma, which means "natural law," or "absolute truth."

As long as time remains to me, I would like to continue teaching the Dharma. I would like to help all those who want to know about them to experience the meditative absorptions. These are levels of consciousness that are entirely different from those people are accustomed to. Through them it is possible to learn to understand religion on a level of profundity that is completely unattainable without meditation.

People who come to me to hear what I have to say, people who attend my seminars and courses, do not have to be or to become Buddhists. The Buddha never used this word. He said, we are practitioners, practitioners in the realm of knowledge.

Whether a person is a Catholic, Protestant, Muslim, Jew, or Hindu is a matter of indifference to me. I don't divide people into such affiliations, which separate them from each other even more than they are already. As long as we think, "I'm this one thing, and you are another," we are not together. But this is a false path. In reality we are all together in the great family of humanity.

The Buddha only had one interest: to show every human being how he or she can become absolutely happy. He never sought disciples and followers. This is my approach also. Whether visitors describe themselves as Catholic or atheist is of no importance. If they are seeking the inner way, I want to help them to find that which lives in all of us—pure peace, pure happiness.

Religion is not confined to any set of traditional cultural or social customs. Such customs are sometimes helpful to people, but they are not the essence of religion. Religion is an inner revelation, a response to the need for perfection that we carry within us.

I have read many of the writings of the Christian mystics of the Middle Ages, particularly Meister Eckhart, Johannes Tauler, Heinrich Seuse, Teresa of Ávila, Francisco de Osuna. Especially Teresa's instructions to her nuns in her book *The Interior Castle* made a particular impression on me, for there she describes the meditative absorptions that I teach also—only in her own personal way and connected with visions shaped by Christianity.

I have twice given talks at the Eckhart Society in England that were devoted to the ideas to be found in common in the teaching of the Buddha and in the sermons of Meister Eckhart.

I believe that it has a profound significance that I am again in Germany. My outer journey has gone in a circle; it began here and I have returned here at the end of my life.

The inner journey followed an entirely different path. I began like so many other people and went along with everything in the ordinary way. Profession, children, and grandchildren. Troubles, inspiration, fears—my life contained all those things. But at the end of my inner journey, I arrived at peace and happiness.

I am very glad that I am able to pass along something of that. I have authorized nine of my students in Germany to teach so that the lost art of the meditative absorptions can continue to exist and not disappear again. In addition to them, I have authorized four teachers in Australia and one in America.

One year after my arrival in Buddha-Haus, Charlie went back to Munich and got married, and he is working again as a tennis coach. Gudrun, after almost eight years as secretary at Buddha-Haus, has left. New forces have taken over: Traudel, who has a degree in mathematics and is a computer programmer, has taken over our bookkeeping, takes care of our banking, our catalogs, and the setting and printing of my books in our own publishing operation.

As for cooking, we have helpers here in Buddha-Haus. We are vegetarian and very undemanding. What is put on our tables is simple and healthy and prepared with love.

We are like a small business that has to be very well organized. The telephone has to be answered, the mail has to be replied to, orders for various things we need have to be sent out.

The cleaning work in the house is for the most part taken on by our course participants and guests. Mornings always have an hour of "selfless helping" scheduled into them that is used for this purpose.

We finance our livelihood and our publications

The ordination of Nyanabodhi. He was the first Buddhist monk to be ordained in the German language.

through donations, course fees, and the sale of tapes (recordings of my talks) and books. Everyone who joins in our common life here renounces any personal income. Our "business" pays for our public health payments and provides a small amount of pocket money for each person.

So much for our organization. Fortunately I have a certain talent for this and also plenty of practice at it. In monasteries and seminaries, order must prevail. One cannot have one's head free for spiritual things and at the same time be surrounded by chaos. Moreover, our outer environment is a mirror image of our inner being.

Roland, the interior designer from Rosenheim who set up our biological sewage system and many other things here, and who creates the images for the jackets of my books in German, has from the first moment been the good spirit of the Buddha-Haus. In 1993 he decided to become a monk. I ordained him along with an Indian monk from Ladakh who was visiting us. I translated the text of the ordination ceremony into German and also recited it in the traditional Pali. It was a moving celebration. His whole family was present.

From that day on, Roland has been called Nyanabodhi. He is the first German monk who also received his ordination in German.

In 1993 I finally did have to undergo a serious cancer operation. The lump, whose growth I could constantly feel, broke open. This was not only very painful but it also bled almost continuously.

Before this operation took place, for all intents and purposes I had finished the business of my life. In order not to leave behind any difficulties or bad feelings, I wrote letters to everyone with whom I had ever had any kind of major or minor disagreement, no matter how far back in time it lay. I apologized for errors of whatever kind that I had committed either knowingly or unknowingly and assured each person that I thought of him or her with love. I felt then that there was nothing that stood in the way of a peaceful death.

After the operation, there were two days during which I had the feeling that my vitality was ebbing away, or more precisely, that it was flowing away through the soles of my feet. I was absolutely reconciled to this, ready to die, and I gave myself over entirely to the pleasant feeling of letting go.

Then a great many cards and flowers from my students arrived that not only showed love but also told me that I should now just stay alive—I didn't need to teach anymore. That made a deep impression on me and encouraged me a lot. In the visits the doctors made and in the care the nurses gave me, I clearly perceived what a great effort they were making to keep me alive. At that point I resolved to help them succeed in this.

Against all expectations, I recovered very nicely. After that, I had three further operations, the last one in November of 1995. During this operation, a strange thing occurred. Although I was fully anesthetized at all times, I suddenly heard an unknown doctor saying, "Oh, for God's sake, something has to be done immediately!" I saw him clearly before me, although my eyes were tightly closed. I saw him trying without success to get a needle into one of my veins and in the process getting more and more nervous. I tried to infuse him with calmness.

The other doctors who were standing around me were becoming impatient, which of course contributed further to the nervousness of the anesthesiologist. He then switched his efforts to my right hand and found a vein, which, with a sigh of relief, he found usable. It was clear to me that my blood pressure had gone down tremendously. I heard someone say "eighty over fifty" and that this was life-threatening. I was also clearly aware that my body was lying there entirely numb and that in the meantime my mind had separated from my body and was watching the whole proceeding from a bird's-eye view. My mind was absolutely calm. I only felt bad for the doctors, and I wanted to help them attain calmness as well.

Everything that I have lived through from this time on and that I continue to live through is, so to speak, a bonus. To have finished with life and then still to be there for a period of time, now already four years longer, and to be able to finish some last things—that is without doubt a great gift.

I am careful to use the time that remains to me very selectively; I only do things now that seem to me valuable and useful. That does not mean that I would indulge in any luxury. I seek to do only what strengthens myself and others inwardly and what brings joy because it is connected with the truth and is helpful.

In 1993 we were discovered by the media. First we were discussed on the Zweites Deutsches Rundfunk, a major German TV network, then there was an article on page three of the *Süddeutschen Zeitung*, a major South German daily newspaper, "portraits" of me on various channels, talks on the radio, and so on. A special gift for me was a phone call from the daughter of our chauffeur in my childhood, who had seen a program about me on television and had nearly fallen over in a faint when she saw a photograph of her father on the screen. She then went so far as to do a meditation course with me. What gave me the most joy was that she remembered my parents. Apart from her, there is very likely no one left in Germany who knew them. She knew how generous and ready to help others my parents always were.

By the major resonance in the public generated by these television programs, we can tell that the teaching of the Buddha, particularly here in the West, is as fresh and authentic, even after twenty-five hundred years, as it ever was and touches the hearts of a great number of people.

We sometimes hear from Asian Buddhists that Western people have difficulty in meditating. That is completely untrue. I have seen through my students—and I have been teaching now for twenty-two years—that they are capable of learning and practicing meditation quite well in every respect. Whoever really devotes himself to meditation can, after some time, experience his or her mind as concentrated and collected on a single point.

I teach various methods. For instance, I show how to be mindful of the breath or by what means it is possible to become aware of and direct one's thoughts. In addition I teach walking meditation and the "piece by piece" method. The latter has to do with feelings and sensations and is an important aid in the purification of our emotions. A further central practice is loving-kindness meditation, for which I use the most varied visualizations to make an opening of the heart possible for everyone. In my courses, I provide guidance in contemplative practices that can open a way to our inner reality. With the help of these traditional methods, the mind gradually becomes calm and temporarily lets go of the world.

The most important teaching, which I am more or less alone in teaching in Europe, is the instructions for the meditative absorptions, which, however, are only possible in a state of complete concentration. In Asia too, as well as in the United States and in Australia, only my students and two other teachers even speak of the absorptions at all. But these absorptions are the real meditation. They were taught by the Buddha; he practiced and praised them highly. They bring the mind to new levels of consciousness, which broaden our horizons and make possible for us a glimpse of the cosmic process. They are the means to the goal of absolute freedom from stress, pressure, and egotism, and they prepare the way to enlightenment.

Every person who practices with patience reaches a

A week-long course in the Dominican monastery of Saint Albert with 170 participants. I am sitting all the way at the rear in the middle.

state of complete concentration. In this way, that person finds a way into the inner space of his or her mind, where absolute purity and clarity prevail. We are then all at once in a position to be able to look objectively at ourselves and the problems that so often threaten to overwhelm us. Through the experience of new levels of consciousness, a new field of vision opens that reveals the world to us anew.

In our meditation room at the Buddha-Haus, we have a larger-than-life-size statue of the Buddha made of teak. It is approximately two hundred years old and comes from Thailand, though it was bought in Kempten, the main city of the Allgäu. It is ornamented with gold leaf, which in Buddhist countries is a traditional way of showing veneration. Next to this statue is where I sit when I give a talk. "I would like to speak to you," I might begin, for example, "about the three marks of existence—about suffering, impermanence, and insubstantiality."

By the stillness of the audience, its attention, I sense its readiness to follow the inward path, the path to the primal truths that the restless, stress-plagued people of today so easily lose track of. In our materialistic world, the meaning of life has become completely unclear for a great number of people, and they content themselves with the satisfaction of the senses, without ever being made happy by it.

One of the great teachers of our time was a monk from Thailand, Ajahn Chah. He had many Western students and died just a few years ago. He used to describe the three marks of existence—suffering, impermanence, and insubstantiality—by means of a simile.

"Look here at this water glass," he would say. "It is very useful for me. I can drink out of it. When the sun shines on it, it breaks up its rays into a display of beautiful colors. When I bang it with a spoon, it gives out a beautiful sound. But when it falls to the ground, it is destroyed. For me, it is already destroyed now. For me, everything that is and that will be has already happened."

This simile is very meaningful for me. My water glass is also already broken. In 1993, for me, my life had already come to an end. Now it is still there, my body is there again, and I use it, but it has just as little meaning for me as a broken glass.

In anything that I do since that time the sense of a personal relationship to it has been missing. I do things presuming that they are helpful. I take pleasure in being able to see these things develop for a little while longer. But when soon this comes to an end, nothing important will have taken place. Everything has already happened anyway.

The Buddha once said that the Dharma would take root in a country when sons and daughters of good families were ordained in their mother tongue. "Good family," however, has nothing to do with wealth or fame. It refers to families in which children learn how to behave with virtue.

Since traveling has become burdensome for me, I am often accompanied by Nyanabodhi. This was the case when I went to California for the wedding of my oldest grandchild, Matthew, when I went to give a meditation course in San Francisco, and when I went to Berlin, where in the summer of 1995, in the framework of the Peace University, I gave a great number of talks; and also when I went to Lindau to the psychotherapy weeks there, where over the last two years I have given talks and workshops.

The great resonance engendered by our work brought me to the idea of opening a city center in Munich. We located a suitable place, a former grocery store with a small apartment attached to it in Neuhausen, a very pleasant part of the city. Now that we have entirely renovated it, it has become a meeting place with a fixed daily program. My students teach there, including Charlie and Norbert. One evening a week, Traudel gives a yoga lesson there; she has been trained in that.

But I still had another vision that I wanted very much to realize before my death: to found in Germany a forest monastery in our Theravada tradition, in a secluded place, so that it could provide a counterpoise to our loud world, overflowing with distractions.

For a while we looked in the Bavarian Forest for a

In front of the Buddha-Haus urban center in Munich, which was opened in 1994. A meditative place for all who wish to escape the hectic life of the city from time to time.

suitable property. And we found one too; but the building regulations were so difficult that after months of struggling back and forth we had to give up on it.

Then in August of 1995 we found the ideal place, quite near us, only a half an hour away from Buddha-Haus. It is at an altitude of one thousand meters, at the foot of the Alps, and on beautiful days you can see the snow-covered peaks of the range quite clearly before you. It consists of seven and a half hectares of meadow and forest, with a stream, a wonderful pure spring, and a house with fourteen bedrooms, all alone in the middle of the landscape.

The house was three hundred years old, a former inn, but it seemed to be in a very tumbledown state. It

Metta Vihara in the Allgäu, the first German forest monastery for Buddhist monks and nuns. The renovation work is almost completed.

had belonged to old people who were no longer able to take care of it. A bank then put it up for obligatory auction. We acquired the premises not exactly cheaply, but still at an advantageous price.

You reach the house by a private road, which is not plowed in winter. Thus we had to get a snowmobile to travel the last kilometer and a half. In this region it often still snows in April. I have often gone in the snowmobile, a kind of motorcycle on skis. I really had to hold on tight, but it was great fun.

Since October of 1995, we have been busy renovating the old house from the ground up. It is mainly Nyana-bodhi who is occupied with this, if "occupied" is really the right word for the hard labor he puts in. A new foundation, a new heating system, and new electric wiring all had to be put in. The outer walls were without insulation, the cellar steps were falling down, and it was raining into the cellar. New drainage ditches had to be dug around the house, and all the rain gutters had to be replaced.

Now Nyanabodhi lives only there. Fortunately, among my students there are some professional tradesmen who charge us only half their normal rate to work there, and there are a number of students that just volunteer their help for days or weeks. Nevertheless, of course the project still costs a lot of money. But on the whole we are quite confident about what we are doing. Looking back over my life shows me that whatever one does earnestly and yet not for one's own gain always works.

Around the house we had to fell a lot of trees to let in air and light and to make room for a garden. A real monastery will always have a garden with flowers, herbs, and a small pond.

We think this place has become the most beautiful forest monastery that could ever be imagined. Moreover, it is the first Buddhist forest monastery in Germany. It is called Metta Vihara ("residence of unconditional love"). This summer (1997) is the opening ceremony. The monastery offers people the possibility to withdraw into silence, into noble silence, into the personal experience of just "being." "Monasticism by installment" arrangements are offered for a minimum of one month.

Of course it is also possible to become a monk or a nun there, after having lived there for at least a year and having concluded that one would like to make inner spiritual growth one's absolute priority in life.

Matthias, now Nyanacitta, a former lawyer from Konstanz on Lake Constance, has become Nyanabodhi's right hand and helps in all areas, from painting the doors to building furniture, from shopping trips to visits to youth groups and a teaching job in the city. For his first year of practice, he officially took the *anagarika* vow and in June he will be ordained as a novice.

As long as I can, of course I too will be at the monastery and teach there. Be that as it may, at the moment we are mainly discussing what colors the doors should be painted and how the cellar walls should be cemented. At the moment these are burning questions.

I am very glad that I was still able to begin this project and will go on to see it completed. For the past twenty years I have had the feeling that I am not directing myself but am being directed—in the direction I have to go in so as to do what I'm supposed to do. And so I also think that I am in the right place at the right time and am bringing about here in Germany something for which there is a growing need.

Not in the air, not in the midst of the sea,
Not in clefts in the rock of mountains,
Not anywhere on this earth can one find
    a place
Where one may abide and death not
    take one.
—Dhammapada, verse 128

A Good Death

Death is something I take for granted. I am prepared to disappear.

The surgeon who operated on me told me once that he admired me. What for, really? Just because the thought of death doesn't cast me into despair?

I always take the Buddha as my example— in both his life and his death, which I hold up before me as an ideal.

Twenty-five hundred years ago, he was born as a king's son in the north of India. His father was the ruler of one of the larger provinces. At his birth, it was prophesied that he would be either an important king or would withdraw from the worldly life and become a buddha. "Buddha" means the awakened one. That is his title. As a prince, he was called Siddhartha Gautama. In addition to the historical data, his life is surrounded by many legends.

The father, we are told, wanted his son to be his successor instead of renouncing the world. And so the world was made to appear as attractive as possible to the boy and then to the young man. It was forbidden for sick or dead people ever to be seen in the palace. Even dead leaves were painstakingly removed to spare Siddhartha the sight of them.

Everything was done for his pleasure. This can in fact be compared with our society of affluence, in which we constantly do everything for our pleasure. Houses, television, videos, telephones, radios—everything is set up for our diversion, so that we can enjoy ourselves. The fact that in this manner in the long run we come to experience no real joy is another matter.

Siddhartha had many male companions as well as female companions who became his concubines. When he was sixteen years old, he was allowed to choose to marry whomever he wished. He chose one of his female cousins. The couple lived in the palace and never had to see anything that might have made them unhappy.

This is similar to the way we hide our own sick and handicapped people behind walls where nobody sees them; and the dead we nicely embalm so that they look good before we bury them.

One day Siddhartha told his chariot driver that he wanted to take a little excursion outside, in front of the palace. They drove outside, and the first thing they saw was a very old man who was supporting himself on a crutch and could barely walk anymore.

"Why does he look so horrible?" asked Prince Siddhartha. The chariot driver, Channah, said, "That is an old man." "Is the same thing going to happen to all of us?" asked the prince. "Of course," said Channah. "We all get old."

They drove back to the palace, and the next day they made another excursion. This time they saw a sick man lying on the street. He was too weak to drink from the water jar that was next to him. Flies were perched on his face, and he could do nothing but moan.

"What's the matter with him?" asked Siddhartha.

"That is a sick person."

"Will we all get sick this way?"

"No one of us is proof against it," said Channah.

The third person, whom Siddhartha saw the following day, was a dead man. He was being carried on a litter, and behind him walked his entire family and all his acquaintances lamenting and crying. The women had strewn ashes in their hair. They were on their way to the cremation ground. "Will we all go there?" the prince wanted to know. "Yes," said Channah, "this awaits all of us."

On the fourth day, Siddhartha drove outside the palace grounds once more. This time he met a man whose face had a peaceful and carefree expression.

"Who is that?"

"That's a monk who has renounced the world," said Channah.

Siddhartha Gautama drove home again, and on the very same night he left his wife, his newborn child, his parents, and his palace and set out to find an answer to the suffering of humanity. In the company of Channah, he rode to the border of his father's kingdom. There he gave Channah his horse and said, "Take it back home and take care of it well."

According to the legend, the horse only went a short stretch of the way back before it fell over and died of a broken heart.

The prince then cut off his hair with his sword, went into the forest, and sought out a well-known teacher of meditation. Until he became the Buddha, he practiced very intensively for six years. After he had completely mastered the meditative absorptions, he sat down under the famous Bodhi Tree in what is now Bodh Gaya and attained the freedom of enlightenment. He formulated the Four Noble Truths and the steps of the Noble Eight-fold Path, which make up the heart of his teaching.* The highest of the Brahmas, the supreme gods, appeared to him as an inner vision and requested him to teach humanity.

It would be beyond our scope here to talk about all the details of this story. In my book *Buddha ohne Geheimnis* (Buddha without mystery) they are spelled out.

Even in an abbreviated form, this story from the life of the Buddha shows what the Buddhist teaching is based on. We have to recognize *dukkha*, which is the Pali word for suffering, worry, lack of fulfillment, sickness, and death. By doing so, we see through the illusions that we have about our "ego" and our life.

----

*The first Noble Truth: Existence is *dukkha* (suffering, absence of fulfillment).
The second Noble Truth: The cause of all *dukkha* is desire.
The third Noble Truth: There is total freedom from *dukkha,* known as *nibbana* [Sanskrit: *nirvana*].
The fourth Noble Truth: The path to absolute freedom is the Noble Eightfold Path.

We cannot achieve this by means of our five senses and our usual way of thinking. For this, another level of consciousness is necessary, which we can attain in the meditative absorptions—in concentration without thought.

In this way we see that we do not exist separately from the rest of creation. And seeing this, we can be freed from the unrelenting craving for recognition, love, respect, and confirmation. Then, at that point, it is no longer so important to us whether we are there or not. We then no longer have any fear of death.

For all this to happen, we only have to let go of something that is quite stubborn—our ego.

We live, we die like all those before us and all those after us, and nothing belongs to us. When we succeed in having no more desires, no more wishes, then death is not annihilation, but rather dissolution into *nibbana* (nirvana).

In order to make this attitude into something real within oneself, we must continue to practice.

In the summer after my operation, I received a lot of visits. My daughter Irene came from America. We took a trip to Italy together. It was the first time in more than twenty years that we'd been alone together. Before that, the children had always been there. There had never been an opportunity for us to talk properly. We took a room in a hotel in Lago Maggiore and took boat trips and went on walking tours. We had time and peace. It was a very, very good thing.

Then I received a visit from Gerd, my divorced husband. He wanted to know how I was. That also, of course, was very nice. We hadn't seen each other since 1979. He came here and immediately busied himself in the garden. It was a pleasure for me to see that he was just the same as ever—always in action, always in motion.

Matthew, my oldest grandchild, visited me with Lara, to whom he is now married. I have a particularly close relationship with him. Of the whole family, he is the one who perhaps has the greatest understanding of his grandmother who became a Buddhist nun.

This reminds me of the fact that in my childhood, I loved my grandfather with particular tenderness. I find that the relationship between the oldest and youngest members of a family is an important thing. It is good to know who came before you and who is coming after you.

Jeff arrived from Australia with his wife and his little daughter. They wanted without fail to see Venice. So we went there, but unfortunately the weather was very bad. Anyhow they saw all the sights while I looked after the little one. Jeff, the one who was with us on all our journeys and, strangely, can remember so little of it all! They stayed for my birthday.

On August 25, 1993, I was seventy years old. It was a nice celebration with lots of laudatory speeches, as is usual on such occasions.

From Nyanabodhi, I got a very special gift: a stupa he had built himself. A stupa is a Buddhist reliquary shrine in the form of a round white tower. This one had a big piece of crystal on the top. On my birthday, we consecrated the stupa.

An opening has been left in the wall. All those who celebrated this day with me were able to put a small Buddha statue inside, which they had received by way of rec-

My eldest grand-child, Matthew, Irene's son, has come from California to visit Buddha-Haus and is participating in his first meditation course. Here we are in the Buddha-Haus garden.

ognition for a donation they had made to Buddha-Haus. A copy of each of my books is preserved inside the stupa. In addition, we put everything we had in the way of gold and other valuables inside. On top of those things. Nyanabodhi put in his dead father's gold wedding band. We didn't have a large number of valuables, but whatever we had we put in the stupa.

One day my ashes will be in there too. That is the traditional way to bury a teacher. Out of caution, I have already applied to the health department in Sonthofen for the necessary permit. There were two functionaries present, who checked through everything and issued a written permit.

With my grandchildren David and Sarah, Jeffrey's children, in Brisbane, Australia.

My seventieth birthday celebration at Buddha-Haus (Jeffrey at far left).

It is a marvelously beautiful place where the stupa stands, next to a small apple tree on a meadow that slopes gently down from that point. When the sun shines, its rays are broken up by the transparent crystal on its tip. I am fond of sitting on the little bench next to it.

There was another event that brought me a lot of joy. After an article about me in a German magazine called *Brigitte*, letters arrived from completely unexpected quarters. Two girlfriends of mine from school, the State Augusta Lyceum in Berlin, wrote me. We used to go to school together when we were between nine and thirteen years old. One wrote from Berlin, another from Heidenheim. The second one even made arrangements for me to give a talk in Heidenheim, to which about three hundred and fifty people came. Then the friend from Berlin enabled me to locate my best friend from school, who lives in England. Perhaps we'll meet this year, when I teach in England.

At the moment I feel quite well for my age. As long as I'm still here, it's fine with me. If I die, that's fine with me too.

My encounter with death has definitely contributed to my ability to propagate the Teaching in a way that has nothing to do with my own person. I am not only unimportant, but I experience myself as not present at all, except as a mouthpiece for things that might help people.

I will live as long as it is determined that I should do so. By now nearly everything has been completed. There are one or two books I would like to see through to completion, especially the *Middle Collection* of the Buddha's discourses, which is urgently in need of a new German translation. Then everything can go on without me.

The stupa in the garden of Buddha-Haus. Here my ashes will be preserved.

In this chapter I am writing a great deal about death, because fear of death is a theme so frequently brought up to me by people who hear my talks. I am continually confronted with this subject. Until we have fully accepted our own death and related to it lovingly and with devotion, our life is bound up with fear. True peace can only enter our hearts when we see things the way they really are.

The Buddha gave a few instructions for relating to the dying, which can be quite helpful. Most important is the following: When a person is dying, we should recall to him all his good deeds, so that he can die with a peaceful and happy mind. That is very important, for it very often occurs that on their deathbeds people are suddenly afflicted with regret and remorse, because they think they have done one thing or another wrong. If you, as a doctor or nurse, do not know a dying person very well, you should get information from his family so you can help him.

We should get in physical contact—hold hands with the dying person or stroke him, so he does not get the feeling he has been abandoned.

The sense of hearing is the last sense to go. Therefore we should not think that a person who seems to be lying there unconscious is not hearing anything. In his presence, only those things should be said that he should hear.

If the dying person is a Buddhist, has faith in the Buddha, and loves his Teaching, verses of his that have been handed down should be recited. There are a few of them that are wonderfully well suited to this purpose. For example:

"Even the magnificent chariot of a king decays; this body too is hastening toward decay. But the Law of the Noble Ones never decays. Noble ones proclaim it through noble messengers." This means that we can say to the person that we all are going to die. The body is not the most important thing. The mind and consciousness of the good and true are much more important. They are not subject to decay.

Death is nothing more than a crossing over. We cross quite gently into a new kind of existence. Of course death only occurs gently if we do not rebel against it—and if we are not in pain.

For a period of time, Buddhist teachers would say that a person should die in a state of full conscious and that for this reason, no painkillers should be given to a dying person. This does not correspond at all to what the Buddha meant when he said that a person should die with a peaceful mind. How can one be peaceful if one is ridden with pain? The Buddhist way of caring for the dying also involves relieving or eliminating pain. If it is necessary for this purpose to render someone unconscious, that is no argument against pain relief. Consciousness is also present even when a dying person cannot answer or respond in the usual way. It is completely wrong to give a person over to pain—this only fills the person's mind with negativity and discord.

And then there is another piece of advice from the Buddha. It is said that one should wait up to three days before burying the body, because the consciousness needs time to separate itself from the body it belongs to.

Buddhist care for the dying also indicates that one should die at home in a good, familiar environment. One's dear ones should be present and know that they have to give the dying person permission to die. It is important to say to him or her: "Yes, we'll miss you, but we're all completely okay, we're just fine. We love you, but we can go on living." We should not try to hold on, since that makes dying more difficult.

I think these are all things that are done the same way in the Christian hospice movement.

Some time ago, a journalist came to us at Buddha-Haus. She asked me if perhaps the reason I was able to accept my death so easily was that I believed in rebirth. "No," I answered her, "I don't hope for that. One is only reborn when the will to be reborn is present. When there is no longer the desire to exist as an ego, then everything is over. I'm ready to let go once and for all."

"And what happens then?" she wanted to know. "Nothing. All over. At that point, *nibbana,* absolute peace, has been attained."

The last great, perfect absorption.

Thanks

First I would like to express many thanks to Ursula Lebert for putting together a publication-ready manuscript for my autobiography from the tape recordings I made. Our mutual understanding contributed in a major way toward making the work easier.

Then my heartfelt thanks to Mr. Graf from the Barth Verlag, whose patience, especially in the choosing of a title, and steady willingness to help was a great aid in bringing this project to completion.

I would further like to thank Traudel, who came up with the final title and made many other good suggestions besides.

Without Nyanabodhi's help in choosing the photos, I never would have gotten through that. Many thanks!

Nyanacitta practiced constructive criticism, which improved the manuscript. Heartfelt thanks!

And then finally, but with a full heart, my gratitude to all the teachers who accompanied me on my life's path. Without their words of encouragement and teaching my life would have looked quite different.

The first were Gerd, Jeffrey, and Irene. Then Phra Khantipalo, the Ven. Nyanaponika Mahathera, the Ven. Naññarama Mahathera, my students in Australia, the United States, and especially in Germany, whose questions, arguments, and offerings have given me much impetus for thought.

I see myself as a person learning from all the human beings I meet and from the nature around me. I experience this with a feeling of happiness and of humility vis-à-vis this endlessly great creation.

Ayya Khema
Buddha-Haus im Allgäu